BOEING 747

Ingo Bauernfeind studied history, visual communication, and documentary film at Hawaii Pacific University, Honolulu. At Pearl Harbor, he initiated and completed various museum projects for the U.S.S. Arizona Memorial, the U.S.S. Missouri, the U.S.S. Bowfin Submarine Museum, the National Park Service, and the U.S. Navy. Over the years, he has written 30 books on naval, military and aviation history including a recent one on the supersonic Concorde. He has also directed or co-produced award-winning documentaries for German and American TV networks, as well as producing interactive museum guides for museums in Pearl Harbor and in Germany.

BOEING 747

50 YEARS OF AN AVIATION ICON

Ingo Bauernfeind

TEMPEST
BOOKS

INTRODUCTION

The Queen Mother of Aviation

As the 'Queen of the Skies', the Boeing 747 began enchanting her worldwide passengers and fans in 1970. Decades later she has lost none of her charm - quite the contrary. Over the course of her successful, eventful, and unique career, the jet has carried the equivalent of almost the entire world's population.

When I flew across the Atlantic to the United States on a Boeing 747 for the last time (to date) in November 2018, it was not as yet foreseeable that the Coronavirus crisis would not only define our lives less than a year and a half later, but also have a huge impact on international air travel.

When the year 2020 dawned, the 747, the Jumbo, had already been in active service for five decades. By then, however, it was already becoming apparent that the Age of the Jumbo - at least as a passenger aircraft - was gradually approaching its final stage, as more cost-effective twin-engine airliners such as the Boeing 777, the 787, and the Airbus A350 were increasingly taking over the role once reserved for the Jumbo. However, no one could have predicted that the Coronavirus crisis and the resulting slump in global air traffic would abruptly force airlines to cut costs. Thus, the end of the Age of the Jumbo accelerated, as many airlines that had been gradually phasing out their planes now had to retire their entire 747 fleet all at once.

Thus, this icon of aviation was deprived of its well-deserved twilight years. Even though the 747 will continue to fly as a freighter, only a few of the passenger variant will still be in service in the coming years.

Regardless of this - or perhaps precisely because of it - it makes sense look back at the more-than-five decades in which the Jumbo has not only left a lasting mark on civil aviation, but has also been successfully deployed in many other roles. Among the numerous aircraft types that have taken to the skies over the years, few have proven as durable and, above all, as versatile as the Jumbo.

This book therefore covers not only the impressive history of the airliner, but also in detail the various variants that have been used in the service of governments, the military, and in the name of science or research, and continue to do so today.

As the 747 has not only permanently changed international aviation over the past decades, but has also influenced numerous new aircraft types, she is not only the Queen of the Skies, but also the *Queen Mother* of all modern widebody jets.

Mülheim, May 2021

THE JET THAT MADE THE WORLD A SMALLER PLACE

The Boeing 747 became synonymous with affordable air travel to faraway places, taking millions of people to sunny beaches in exotic lands. It was able to fly more passengers farther than any other aircraft before it.

CHAPTER 1

On September 30, 1968, thousands of people gathered at the brand-new Boeing plant in Everett, some 30 miles north of Seattle, Washington, on the U.S. West Coast. The occasion was the presentation, known as the rollout, of a new passenger aircraft from the renowned aircraft company Boeing. This was not just a simple premiere in front of the public, as it often was – it was the first appearance of the Boeing 747, the largest passenger aircraft in the world, which was to leave a lasting mark on aviation. More than that, it was also to redefine the shape and size of airports and make an enormous contribution to global cargo aviation.

The 1960s were marked by unrest, change, but also new beginnings: young people were rebelling against their parents, the U.S. and the Soviet Union were engaged in their race to the moon, the conflict in Vietnam was raging, and Cold War tensions between East and West were everywhere.

Thanks to various technological advances during this turbulent decade, international air travel, which until then had been virtually a privilege of the wealthy because of its high cost, gradually evolved into a way of transportation that benefitted the less well-off. An important key to this change was a new generation of jet-powered aircraft. These were larger and faster than their propeller-driven predecessors. Thanks to their powerful engines, they could climb higher and even fly over bad weather instead of having to dodge storms in a time-consuming detour. This shortened flight times to distant destinations, in some cases enormously.

Boeing's 707 passenger jet became a mainstay in the growing fleets of international airlines in the late 1950s. It was joined by various competing models of British, French, and Soviet production. While the ever-larger jets could carry more passengers, this meant that international airports also had to grow to keep up with demand. The actual idea for a new aircraft that would dwarf previous passenger jets came not from Boeing itself, but from one of its customers.

The 747 has captured the imagination of travellers from around the world. (Boeing)

During his four decades at the helm of Pan American World Airways, its president, Juan Trippe, had repeatedly set new standards, both for his company and for the airline industry. This successful strategy had enabled Pan Am to become a leader, if not *the* leader, among the world's airlines since the era of the great flying boats, the advent of international air travel after 1945, and the dawn of the jet age in the 1950s. Trippe observed increasing congestion at international airports in the early 1960s. While the number of flights was growing steadily, the aircraft of the time could themselves carry only a relatively small number of passengers. A larger jet with more seats, on the other hand, could help airlines reduce the cost per passenger carried. Although several supersonic transports (SSTs) were still in development, and had been for years, Trippe wanted a large jet in a timely manner that could meet the capacity requirements.

Thus, the history of the world-famous Jumbo can be traced in part to the president of Pan Am, but also to a now almost-forgotten U.S. Air Force request for proposals. In the early 1960s, the air force began taking delivery of the Lockheed C-141 Starlifter. This large four-engine jet could carry 28 tonnes of cargo over distances of about 3,500 miles (5,600 kilometres). It became apparent, however, that the air force would soon need an even larger transport aircraft.

In spring of 1964, therefore, U.S. aircraft manufacturers received a request for submitting their designs. The new freighter was to be capable of carrying 115,000 pounds (52 tonnes) of cargo over a maximum distance of 5,000 nautical miles (9,260 kilometres). In addition, the cargo hold was to be 17 feet (5.18 metres) wide, 13.5 feet (4.1 metres) high, and 100 feet (30 metres) long, so that an army tank in particular could comfortably embark. In addition, the aircraft was to have front and rear loading ramps so that vehicles could enter or exit at either end.

In addition to Boeing, other well-known manufacturers such as Lockheed, Douglas, General-Dynamics, and Martin-Marietta

A Boeing 707 in service with Air France. Launch customer was Pan Am in 1958. (Air France Museum)

submitted their designs for a large cargo aircraft. Each of them worked on a solution to the central question: where can the cockpit be placed if the flip-up cargo door is to be integrated into the nose of the aircraft? For example, while Douglas's design called for some sort of cockpit pod on top of the fuselage in front of the wings, Lockheed wanted to place the cockpit, with a cabin for additional passengers behind it, in a long 'spine' that extended almost the entire length of the aircraft. Boeing's concept lay somewhere between these other two proposals and would later prove to be a wise decision regarding the Jumbo's design.

In the end, the Lockheed company was able to win the tender for the transport aircraft. Their design, later designated the C-5 Galaxy, entered air force service in 1970 and would remain the largest aircraft in the world until the first flight of the Soviet Antonov An-124 in 1982. Although Boeing suffered defeat in this important bidding process, its (rejected) concept would soon be used to develop another aircraft that would make history as the 747.

The U.S. engine manufacturer Pratt & Whitney had also lost the bid for the C-5, but had developed a new, very large engine with a thrust of over 180 kN (40,000 lbf). And because Juan Trippe suspected that he would have to wait for years for a real SST, he wanted a commercial aircraft that was

The Lockheed C-5 Galaxy is distinguished by its flip-up cargo hatch in the nose. The cockpit is located above it. (U.S. Air Force)

gigantic by the standards of the time, twice the size of the Boeing 707 with its 180–219 seats. So, Juan Trippe again called his friend Bill Allen, president of Boeing, as he had done in the case of the successful 707.

"Bill Allen was one of the greatest CEOs of the 20th century," says Michael Lombardi, the senior corporate historian for the Boeing Company since 1994. "He understood the aviation business very well. At the time the SST was considered the future of commercial aviation and naturally Boeing had to compete for it. The 747 was something that was requested by Juan Trippe and since Pan Am was one of Boeing's leading customers (and the other airlines followed Pan Am's lead), this made it important for Boeing to build the 747."

In 1965, Boeing president Bill Allen appointed one of his leading engineers, Joe Sutter, to lead the 747 design team under Malcolm T. Stamper, overall leader of the 747 project and later president of Boeing.

After attending college and serving for some time on a destroyer escort during World War II, Sutter was originally offered a position

Joe Sutter after the rollout of the Boeing 747 in 1968. (Boeing)

Joe Sutter, father of the 747, with a 747-8 model. Although retired from Boeing in 1986, he continued to serve the company in an advisory capacity. Even in his 90s, he could often be found in his office at Boeing Commercial Airplanes headquarters, or up at Everett for one reason or another. Sutter was widely hailed as a preeminent senior statesman of aviation and has won many prestigious awards, including having Boeing's 40-87 building at Everett renamed in his honour – the Joe Sutter Engineering Building. (Boeing)

at Douglas Aircraft Corporation. However, he chose to join Boeing instead, even though the job paid $10 less, at $200 per month. His first task at Boeing was the propeller-driven airliner Boeing 377 Stratocruiser. "The Stratocruiser had a lot of problems, so I worked on all kinds of engineering problems," says Joe Sutter.[1] "I learned more about airplanes than those guys working on the jets, and that's what started me as an aeronautical engineer." Sutter is thankful he started on that model, adding, "an airplane is a whole thing, and you have to make the whole thing work right, and I learned a lot on that old airplane." With many lessons learned from his work on the Stratocruiser, he began studying jet-powered aircraft, and was the first Boeing employee to fly to Germany and make a presentation on a jet to Lufthansa. After distinguishing himself through his work on the new 737 short-haul airliner, amongst others, he was given the leadership of the 747 design team. This envisaged the development of a huge commercial aircraft inspired by the air force tender and Juan Trippe's desire for a passenger jet to relieve congestion at airports.

Sutter and his team not only adopted the idea of the high-placed cockpit and flip-up nose, but also Pratt & Whitney's JT9D engine.

After its defeat by the General Electric TF39 as a candidate engine for the Lockheed C-5, its further development as a civilian engine took place. "The JT9D was Pratt & Whitney's offering for the new technology high-bypass turbofan engine," says Boeing historian Michael Lombardi. "General Electric had won the contract to supply engines for the C-5 Galaxy, which meant that Pratt & Whitney could focus on supporting the 747 programme; also, the JT-9D was a more powerful engine with potential for growth."

Joe Sutter, in talking with Pan Am and other potential customers, recognised that many international airlines wanted a jet that could carry far more people than the 180 to 219 passengers of the globally popular 707. Larger aircraft could carry more passengers, reducing the number of jets at airports and the associated traffic and avoiding congestion. In addition, a larger number of passengers per aircraft meant that the cost of transportation per person, and therefore the cost of operation, decreased relative to the size of the jets.

"I had a good team of all kinds of engineers that were studying what we needed to do," says Sutter. "Airlines like Pan Am and Lufthansa knew they needed an airplane bigger than the 707. The market was growing very fast. We visited airlines like Lufthansa discussing the requirements, how big, how far it flies,

This model depicts a double-deck 747. However, since the 747 was built as a widebody jet, it would take until the early 21st century for the later competitor Airbus to produce a commercial double-deck airliner in the form of the A380. (Boeing)

Evacuation exercise with a Swissair Boeing 747. Before being introduced into service, the successful evacuation of 350 passengers had to be demonstrated in 90 seconds. (Swissair, ETH-Bibiothek Zürich/ LBS_SR05-000615-15/CC BY-SA 4.0)

Detailed and walk-through mock-up of an entire cabin section of a Boeing 747. (Boeing)

and what it does look like. Pan Am wanted a double-decker airplane of about 350 seats, that is about two and a half times bigger than a 707. This double-decker idea, the more we looked at it, the more we decided it was not going to go. So very late in the game, we came to our management and said, 'We don't think it's the right kind of airplane.' And after a long struggle we went to what we called a 'wide single deck concept' which resulted in putting a cockpit up above the freighter version of the airplane. But if we had not changed to the wide single-decker there would be no 747 today.

"The double-decker airplane at that time had no cargo capability and no growth capability, and it had a lot of technical problems, too, like emergency egress; we engineers knew all that, but trying to convince management when they didn't want to hear it, was a tough struggle.

"What we did was to build some plywood mock-ups and we invited airline executives, Juan Trippe and the heads of Lufthansa and British Airways, to Seattle, and we just showed them the various concepts, and after they saw the two concepts side by side, they decided the wide single-deck airplane was the right answer. It was a struggle to even build those

Top Right: *Early 747 cabin cross-section mock-up. Full-size cabin replicas like this one eventually convinced customers like Pan Am, Lufthansa and British Airways that a widebody design with one deck was the best concept for transporting 350 passengers. (Boeing)*

Presenting models of the Boeing 2707 SST in 1963. This was the first American supersonic transport (SST) project. After winning a competition for a government-funded contract to build an American SST, Boeing began development at its facilities in Seattle, Washington. The design emerged as a large aircraft with seating for 250 to 300 passengers and cruise speeds of approximately Mach 3. (Boeing)

mock-ups because nobody would give us a budget to build them."[2]

In addition to the technical challenges, however, there was a fundamentally existential problem: at the time, Boeing was feverishly working on a far more ambitious project called Supersonic Transport (SST), a supersonic passenger jet that would outperform the future British–French Concorde and the Soviet Tupolev Tu-144. The 1960s were a promising time for the aircraft industry, as commercial aviation seemed to be moving toward supersonic flight. With many military aircraft now flying faster than sound and some even reaching Mach 2 (twice the speed of sound), it was a logical thought to develop civilian aircraft with similar flight performance. At that time, passenger numbers were increasing by 15 per cent annually and were expected to double by 1980. International cargo flying was also experiencing strong growth rates.

With an eye toward international supersonic air travel, many aviation industry and airline experts assumed that most passengers would prefer the time-saving Concorde, Tu-144, Boeing's SST, or another American supersonic

transport in the future rather than much slower subsonic jets. Thus, in order to secure a long-term future for the Boeing 747, which at the time occupied the role of an underdog among glamorous supersonic projects, it had to be a good cargo plane in addition to its qualities as a passenger aircraft. This desire had a considerable effect on the overall design.

Indeed, Sutter recognised that these large jets would one day be converted to freighters. This meant that the 747 airliner would have to retain the same configuration as the 747 freighter, with the cockpit above the passenger cabin, since Sutter and many others assumed that it would not fly as a commercial airliner for long, but would soon fly only as a freighter. This early realisation later contributed to the Jumbo's long-term success.

In addition to passenger transport, whether supersonic or subsonic, Juan Trippe was also thinking about the cargo business, which was also growing rapidly. The possibility of using standardised cargo containers that could be transported directly from the truck to the aircraft and stowed in pairs side by side in the hold required the design of a widebody aircraft with a much wider fuselage. "One of the great accomplishments of Joe Sutter's team was to create the optimal design that could be both a great passenger plane and an excellent freighter without any compromises," says historian Michael Lombardi. "The features built into the plane to make a freighter, such as

Testing a model for a supersonic airliner in NASA's wind tunnel. (NASA)

Boeing's Bill Allen (left) and Pan Am's Juan Trippe pose for a photo in front of the 747 prototype. Their faith in the new aircraft paid off. (Boeing)

the width of the interior and the upper deck, actually added to the passenger appeal of the airplane." Sutter adds: "I've flown in a lot of 747s, and the beauty of it is that you have zones to put First Class, Business Class, high-fare, expensive passengers, and lower-fare tourists. It has a tremendous amount of flexibility, and that's one of the beauties of the 747, and on top of all that it's got a lot of good freight capability."[3]

Boeing's ambitious SST, known as the 2707, never got beyond the design stage and a full-size mock-up. Horrendous development costs, the heavy financial burdens of the U.S. space programme, and the Vietnam War led the U.S. Congress to finally end government support for the project entirely in 1971. Regardless, SST engineers faced numerous technical problems. In addition, there were

This picture impressively shows the difference in size between the Boeing 707 and the huge 747 behind it. (Boeing)

environmental concerns about the enormous fuel consumption and, not least, about the severe noise caused by sonic booms during flights over populated areas.

The Way Forward

Three days before Christmas 1965, Bill Allen and Juan Trippe signed a letter of intent to build what would become the Boeing 747. "If you build it, I'll buy it" and "If you buy it, I'll build it" were the oft-cited pledges of the two friends.

"The relationship between Allen and Trippe was much more of a friendship than a business relationship, explains Michael Lombardi. "Trippe started Pan Am in 1927

Watch Video: Jumbo News 1966

and in that same year Bill Boeing started Boeing Air Transport, which would become United Airlines. Bill Allen was the attorney for Boeing Air transport, so both men shared a bond of being pioneers of the airline industry."

Even on paper, the specifications for the new behemoth were breathtaking: a gross weight of 500,000 pounds (227 tonnes), a passenger capacity of 350 to 400, a range of 5,100 miles (8,200 kilometres) at full capacity, and a MMO (maximum Mach operating) speed of Mach 0.92 (530 knots or 980 kph) at a cruising altitude of 35,000 feet (10,668 metres). For comparison, the latest Jumbo variant, the 747-8, has a slower MMO of 0.90, which was chosen largely out of convenience as no no airline was known to routinely fly the aeroplane at the 0.92 MMO limit. In addition, the new aircraft was to be quieter than the 707. However, the key specifications in effect at the time the contract was signed were subsequently to change as the aircraft became heavier and longer.

With a value of half a billion dollars (more than $4 billion today), the contract between Boeing and Pan Am was not only the largest deal in the history of civil aviation, but also held great risks for both companies. While Boeing had to build a huge new factory at a cost of $250 million, Pan Am had to come

Since the Renton production plant in Washington was at capacity producing the 707, 727 and 737 models, Boeing had a forest cleared in Everett, about 30 miles (50 kilometres) north of Seattle, and built a factory there: at 1,100 feet (335 metres) long, 295 feet (90 metres) wide and 66 feet (20 metres) high, it would become – and still is – the largest (enclosed) building in the world. (Boeing)

up with half the purchase price for the contractually agreed 25 aircraft before the Jumbo was even certified by the Federal Aviation Administration (FAA).

Thus, the wheels were slowly setting in motion for the 'second jet age'. Everything about the Jumbo was huge: at 231 feet (70.6 metres) long to its tail and with a wingspan of nearly 195 feet (60 metres), it could not be built in any of Boeing's existing facilities. The company had to build an entirely new factory large enough to roll out the brand-new Jumbos at the end. Thus, the world's largest passenger jet also required the construction of the world's largest building for its assembly.

Boeing agreed to hand over the first 747 to Pan Am by the end of 1969. The delivery date left 28 months to develop the aircraft, which was two-thirds of the normal time. The schedule was so fast-paced that Joe Sutter and his team that worked on it were given the nickname 'The Incredibles'.

Developing the aircraft was such a technical and financial challenge that management was said to have 'bet the company' when it started the project. Boeing got involved with the Jumbo during an ambitious phase in its corporate history: during the 1960s, it designed not only this new aircraft and

its production facility, but also the smaller 737 and various systems for NASA's Apollo programme. Boeing also worked on the ill-fated SST until the project was cancelled in 1971. To finance the 747 in particular, Boeing had to take out loans from no fewer than seven banks. For years to come, the financial situation was to remain tight.

"The SST was cancelled while Boeing was already contracting from the worldwide recession that started in 1968," explains Michael Lombardi. "The cancellation of the SST was the final blow in an already desperate situation. Boeing was forced to make drastic cuts and over half of the workforce was let go, the Seattle area had more unemployment at that time than we have seen during the [2020–21 Coronavirus] pandemic – the desperate time led a local real estate company to put up a billboard near Sea-Tac airport that read, 'Will the last person to leave Seattle turn out the lights.' Due to the recession, airlines stopped buying new planes and both the 737 and 747 still had considerable startup costs to recover. This created a great deal of concern about these programmes and their future."[4]

In addition to financial constraints, a shortage of engineering talent was also looming at Boeing. Joe Sutter, who became known as the 'Father of the 747', had to fight to keep from

A mock-up of the 747 during development. The jet had to be designed and built in only 28 months, as opposed to the usual 42 months for a new passenger aircraft. Boeing moved so quickly that the first 747 was under construction at its huge Everett plant before the roof of the building was completed. (Boeing)

Top: *The 747 was not a light jet. Despite Pan Am's strict weight specifications and the relatively high proportion of 11 per cent titanium in the total weight, Boeing was forced to increase the weight by 10 per cent to 322 tonnes. (Boeing)*

Bottom: *Static tests with the 747's wings at the Everett factory in 1969 to determine the load capacity. (Boeing)*

losing his valuable engineers to other projects within the company. With all the ongoing programmes, there was not only a shortage of funding, but also a shortage of engineering talent, as many capable people moved or were transferred to the SST and other projects. Sutter had to do a lot of convincing to get his engineers to keep working on the 747.

"I had 4,500 engineers working for me right at the peak of designing the airplane [the 747]," says Sutter. "I was put under pressure by my management to drop 1,000 engineers. Could you imagine what the hell would have happened to the programme if I did that? It would have been a disaster. And I'll never forget the results of that meeting where I got up and told them I can't give up 1,000 engineers; in fact, my people said they needed 800 more, that's why we're using overtime and weekends. When I walked out of that meeting, nobody would look at me, and I went out in the hall ... Next day I went to work and nobody said a word.

Watch Video: Construction

"If you can have all your engineers in one place, you would do a better job. We had engineers in four or five places, so I was on the road a lot, coordinating. But this business of spreading the workloads all over the world is not the right way to do it. The best thing to do is realise the situation and work like hell to get your job done, which is what we did."[5]

Development and Testing

Testing on numerous components and systems began even before the first 747 was fully assembled. These included load and fatigue testing of numerous components including the huge wings and engines. One important test involved the evacuation of 560 volunteers from a cabin mock-up built in original size via the aircraft's emergency chutes. As such a large aircraft had never been evacuated before, so this test marked entering uncharted territory: the first realistic full-scale evacuation took two and a half minutes instead of the

Flight attendants from 26 airlines that ordered the 747 adorn the prototype on rollout day. (Boeing)

Top: *A 747 fuselage is repeatedly pressurised and depressurised through many thousands of cycles to verify structural integrity. (Boeing)*

Bottom: *Boeing 747 project pilot Jack Waddell in an early cockpit simulator, circa 1967. In 1972, he became Boeing's chief test pilot and, four years later, director of flight training. He retired in 1981. (Boeing)*

huge doors of the Everett factory opened and out rolled the prototype RA001. Its white fuselage with red stripes was adorned with the emblems of 26 airlines, all of which had already signed contracts to purchase the Jumbo, for a total of $1.5 billion (over $11 billion today) The gamble seemed to be

A flight attendant poses in front of one of the four massive engines, probably unaware that it is only a dummy. (SAS Scandinavian Airlines)

Watch Video: Testing

maximum of 90 seconds as required by the FAA, and several volunteers were injured. Subsequent test evacuations met the required 90 seconds but caused more injuries. In 1968, the price tag for the programme had risen to $1 billion ($7.5 billion today).

Rollout

September 30, 1968 marked an important milestone in the history of the Jumbo. Before the eyes of the international press and representatives of the aviation industry, the

paying off for Boeing. Even the night before the rollout, technicians had been feverishly working on the prototype to present the public with what appeared to be a finished aircraft. In reality, the paint had not as yet dried everywhere and the four engine nacelles were fitted with dummy engines, in front of which the flight attendants of future customers posed for photos. The highlight of the day came when the flight attendants christened it *City of Everett*. Historian Lombardi explains the ceremony's significance: "Over time what has proven to be the most memorable part of the rollout was having a flight attendant

Top Left: *Rollout of the first Boeing 747 (RA001) on September 30, 1968. A common reaction upon first seeing the 747 was that it reminded its observers of a majestic ocean liner with wings. The massive jet, almost as long as a soccer field, now had a maximum takeoff weight of 322 tonnes (710,000 lb) and could carry up to 490 passengers. (Boeing)*

Middle Left: *Christening of the jet with champagne by the 26 flight attendants. (Boeing)*

Middle Right: *The prototype's first flight crew: chief test pilot Jack Waddell (left), co-pilot Brien Wygle (centre) and flight engineer Jess Wallick (right). (Boeing)*

Bottom: *The rollout was a major public event attended by the international press and representatives of the aviation industry. (Boeing)*

from each airline that had ordered the 747 to christen the airplane. That was a brilliant idea from the Boeing PR department and the photo of the flight attendants lined up in front of the 747 is one of the most enduring and iconic photos of commercial aviation history."[6]

Watch Video: Rollout

Maiden Flight

After months of preparations and careful planning, the long-awaited maiden flight of the *City of Everett* was set for February 9, 1969. The flight crew consisted of the 747's chief test pilot Jack Waddell, co-pilot Brien Wygle, and flight engineer Jess Wallick. "Our three-man crew was all experienced," says Brien Wgyle. "I am often asked, 'Were you frightened, were you concerned, were you nervous about this first flight?' I want to tell you we were not. Not that we were all that brave … the facts were that we were very happy to finally get this programme going … We had all the confidence in the world. After all, we had a huge respect for the engineering and manufacturing people in the Boeing Company, as we had been flying their products for some time."[7]

Watch Video: First Flight

Born in 1924 in Seattle, Washington, Brien Wygle joined the Royal Canadian Air Force in 1942. During World War II, he was transferred to the China-Burma-India theatre, where he flew over 200 airdrop missions in support of Allied troops. In 1951, he joined Boeing as a test pilot. During his 39-year career with the company, Wygle participated in test flights for

The moment of truth – the 747 prototype takes off on its maiden flight on February 9, 1969. Initially, the Jumbo was not without controversy – while many cheered the jet, many could not imagine it would fly at all, that the 747 was called by some the 'Titanic of the Skies'. According to Brien Wygle, the four Pratt & Whitney JT9D engines each produced only 173.5 kN (39,000 lbf) of thrust instead of the intended 191.3 kN (43,000 lbf). Some 40 engines were being used until the engineers found four good ones that could be used for the maiden flight. (Boeing)

The prototype during its first flight. For safety reasons, the landing gear remained extended during the entire flight. "The crew had emergency parachutes on board," says Brien Wygle. "There was a pole to the cargo hold where the escape hatch/door was. Before the first flight, Jess Wallick went to the Everett fire station to find out what the best technique was to slide down the pole." (Boeing)

numerous Boeing aircraft, including the B-47 Stratojet, B-52 Stratofortress, Model 367-80, 707, 727, 737, and 747. In 1990, he retired as Boeing's vice-president of flight operations.

Brien Wygle vividly remembers the day of the Jumbo's maiden flight: "There was an enormous outpouring of publicity. There was press from all over the world; it was incredible the attention this airplane got. There were customers, there were contractors ... everybody, and television everywhere. So we knew we were being watched.

"However, the weather was not suitable, so we had to delay the flight [set for 10 a.m.] by a couple of hours. But eventually we ventured out; it was not perfect, but it was good enough. Our feeling was one of relief ... we wanted to get on with it. We knew we would take off and land in front of everybody, and even though we were a bunch of engineers and test pilots doing our work very meticulously, I think in view of all that publicity our underlined theme was, 'Don't screw up!'"[8]

Boeing historian Michael Lombardi shares an anecdote: "Before the flight Bill Allen told chief pilot Jack Wadell, 'You know, Jack, I hope you understand the future of the Boeing Company rides with you today.' Jack replied sardonically; 'Well, Bill, thanks a lot – I needed that!'"

Nevertheless, with Jack Waddell at the controls, Brien Wygle in the co-pilot's seat, and Jess Wallick in the flight engineer's seat, the world's largest passenger aircraft finally took

The City of Everett lands safely after its 76-minute maiden flight. The jet was found to be largely immune to 'Dutch roll', a major hazard to early swept-wing jets. This type of aircraft motion consists of an out-of-phase combination of 'tail-wagging' (yaw) and rocking from side to side (roll). (Boeing)

One of the first test aircraft (747-100) during a VMU test takeoff. During a Velocity Minimum Unstick test, the tail of an aircraft is deliberately touched down on a runway just before takeoff. The test helps to determine minimum takeoff speeds for new aircraft. Abrasion protection, such as a dense wooden plank, is attached to the underside of the empennage before the test to protect it from damage. (Boeing)

The tests also involved taxiing the large aircraft on the ground. While the first Jumbos were still under construction, a device was needed to allow pilots to practise taxi manoeuvres from a high upper-deck position. Therefore, an unusual training device consisting of a mock-up cockpit mounted on a truck was built and nicknamed Waddell's Wagon, after 747 chief test pilot Jack Waddell. (Boeing)

off and soared into the skies. Despite a minor problem with one of the flaps, the prototype handled extremely well. For safety reasons, the landing gear had to be extended during the entire flight. This was and remains a standard procedure of minimising risk. Maintaining the takeoff configuration – the flaps also remain extended – minimises exposure to potential changes in handling qualities and the possibility of unexpected systems failures early in the flight. The jet was accompanied by a chase plane, flown by Paul 'Pablo' Bennett. This was and still is standard practice and plays a broad safety role on an aircraft's first flight. For example, one of the many safety-related responsibilities of the chase plane pilot is to monitor the exterior of the test aircraft for signs of malfunctions. After a 76-minute flight, Jack Wadell landed the prototype safely.

"Obviously, during the first flight we did not delve into the difficult corners," recalls Brien Wygle. "But flying the airplane was a delight. It was a pilot's airplane.

"I think the public had more trouble getting used to the size than we in the company did because it seems so large that people found it difficult to believe you could actually put such a thing in the air. And, of course, it turned

During the flight testing, barrels filled with water served as a ballast system to test the centre of gravity on the ground and during flight. The barrels could be moved forward or aft to test the system. (Boeing)

out to be very easy to fly. And it took a little adapting ... because you were so high in the air compared to any other airplane."[9]

Flight Testing and Engine Problems

"There are a number of things that you have to solve in every programme," explains Brien Wygle. "You have to check for flutter, you have to check for stall speeds and stall characteristics, which determine takeoff and landing speeds, and you have to check for the cruise speeds and the fuel burn that accompanies those cruise speeds. Those are the bases of what you are going to go about. Some of the more interesting areas are flutter and stalls."[10]

During the detailed flight test programme, flutter testing showed that, under certain conditions, the Jumbo's massive wings would oscillate, or vibrate. Sutter's engineers were able to solve this problem by changing the stiffness of some wing components.

According to a report composed by Thomas D. Gallacher, radiation safety officer at Boeing, for the Oak Ridge National Laboratory in 1994, depleted uranium (DU) was used as a counterweight in the tailplane of 550 747s produced from between 1968 and 1981. DU helped to redistribute mass and weight as part of the anti-flutter measures as its high density allowed the concentration of relatively high weights in a small area, such as the

interior of a tailplane. Depending on model and configuration, each aircraft had 21 to 31 counterweights in its tail assembly, thus carrying between 692 and 1,059 pounds of DU. This controversial measure caused concern in the event that these jets had were to have an accident. However, since 1981, Boeing has used tungsten counterweights in new 747s and as spares, and returned counterweights to the manufacturers of the counterweights for salvage and recycling, and recommended customer airlines do so as well.

The report further states that, "based on the data from National Lead [a lead smelting company in Houston, Texas], reported in the section on exposures to the general public, dose rates to flight crew will be less than 0.8 microrem per hour. During a 2,000-hour working year, this results in a maximum potential exposure of 1.6 millirem, less than 2 per cent of the 100 millirem per year limit for members of the general public. This is only 1/600th of the 500 microrem per hour increase in dose rate from cosmic radiation flight crew experience at 39,000 feet."[11]

Testing the noise levels generated by a 747-100 during takeoff, early 1970s. (Boeing)

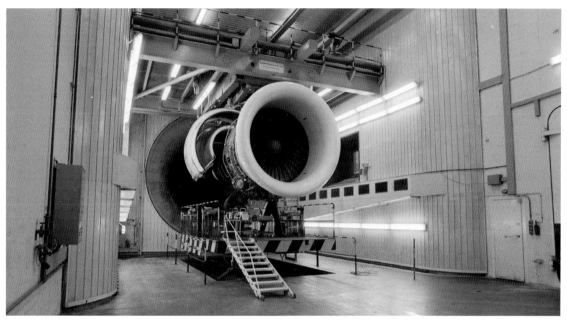

Engine test stand at Swissair during the 1970s. Not only engine manufacturers but also airlines conduct extensive tests on their engines. (Swissair/ETH-Bibliothek Zürich/LBS_SR05-079009A-18A/CC BY-SA 4.0)

"The flying characteristics were never a difficulty," Brien Wygle recalls. "It was very stable on approach; it was a very solid airplane. The wing sweep was greater than it had been on the previous Boeing airplanes and the 747 cruised at a higher Mach number. In flight we actually took it to essentially Mach 0.98, which was just a tiny bit slower than the speed of sound. That was beyond the red line we had to prove, but ... here was this massive airplane and we were taking it to unprecedented speeds."[12]

Flight testing was hampered by problems with the Pratt & Whitney JT9D jet engines, including engine stalls caused by rapid throttle movements and distortion of the turbine casings just after a few hours of flight service. These problems delayed the delivery of the production aircraft to airlines for several months with up to 20 aircraft at the Everett plant stranded while awaiting engine installation. In order to keep the massive aircraft balanced, they had concrete blocks mounted under their wings.

"We had a terrible engine history," says Brien Wygle. "The engines on the 747 were prone to surge, and surging meant that the flow into the engine would break down, and there would be an enormous bang and a temporary loss of thrust. That was something you wanted to avoid. There was a great deal of discussion between Boeing and Pratt & Whitney. But the facts were that they were failing regularly and it wasn't producing the thrust that we wanted. Now, whether that was Pratt's fault or Boeing's fault is another story. But anyway, the point was it was not producing thrust."[13]

Both companies worked feverishly to solve the problem. Jack Waddell even took the president of Pratt & Whitney on a flight and showed him the engine failure in 'real time'. Gradually, the performance and reliability of the JT9D engines improved (see Chapter 2: Design of a Marvel).

"One day, they wanted me to do a maximum weight takeoff," describes Brien Wygle. "As they didn't want to do it on Boeing Field's runway, we flew over to Moses Lake the night before [the test flight]. There we had a long runway, but at this maximum weight, one of the engines failed on me right after takeoff. I struggled to get the engine back, so I could

Damaged fan of a GE engine of a Boeing 747. Many engine elements are subjected to severe stress and wear during operation. (Swissair/ETH-Bibliothek Zürich/LBS_SR05-001263-11/CC BY-SA 4.0)

fly it back into Boeing Field ... It took quite a while at that maximum weight and the low-thrust engines (and with only three of them) to get up to the 10,000 or so feet [that] I needed to cross the Cascades [mountain range] to land back at Boeing Field. So, the history was very checkered in the early days. We had a lot of difficulties. And, of course, looming over us at that time was the fact that the cost of this airplane development was running about double what it had been budgeted. So it was, believe me, a very difficult and demanding time. But I want to point out that, despite the difficulties that we had, we certified the airplane on time and delivered it essentially on time and made up for all those difficulties."[14]

In addition to the first 747 prototype, Boeing built four more aircraft for test and evaluation purposes. After the end of the flight test programme, the company kept only the first aircraft, while the other four eventually became airline jets. The last of these four additional Jumbos, a 747-131 (SF) (No. 5-8101), was the fifth ever built. Today it is the oldest surviving 747 (second only to the prototype), and is still registered in the Iranian Air Force fleet.

European Supersonic Rivals

The difficulties with the engines did not prevent Boeing from taking a 747 to Paris in the summer of 1969 in order to present it to an audience for the first time overseas. "The trip to the Paris Air Show was one of the difficult things," remembers Brien Wygle. "The airplane had only been flying for about four months when Boeing decided to take it to the Paris Air Show. Going there was vital as this was the [747's] first year in flight, and we had to get that airplane to France to sell it. This was an important deal, so we ventured out and our pilots flew it to the Paris Air Show and back without difficulty, but I think Joe [Sutter] and everybody else had their fingers crossed the whole time."[15]

As coincidence would have it, the Anglo-French Concorde, which had made her maiden flight just weeks after the Jumbo, also arrived at Le Bourget, Paris. Both aircraft seemed to be harbingers of an amazing age of aviation. As it turned out, the civilian supersonic aircraft was not to fulfill its early promise, while the Boeing 747 was just at the beginning of what would become a decades-long saga of success. The Concorde programme was suffering various blows. Her sonic boom made supersonic air travel overland practically impossible without causing complaints from people, thus ruining her unique selling point, which was speed, particularly in the United States.

Moreover, various events further dampened Concorde's sales prospects. One of them was the 1973 oil crisis that resulted in soaring fuel prices. Many airlines, which had previously shown interest in the fast but thirsty jet, now became very cautious about aircraft types with a significantly higher fuel consumption than subsonic airliners such as the Boeing 747, which made commercial air travel far more cost-efficient than the Concorde (or any other SST): the Jumbo could transport more than four times more passengers, was much more fuel-efficient and had a much longer range. While the Concorde could just cross the Atlantic, the Jumbo was capable of flying to nearly every destination across the globe including overland routes without the annoying sonic boom.

In such times of economic uncertainty, the subsonic 747 looked like a significantly less

A Concorde takes off. After all other airlines had cancelled their orders for the supersonic jet, it was only put into service by Air France and British Airways. (Air France Museum)

The Soviet SST, the Tupolev Tu-144, which had first taken to the skies in December 1968, was cancelled during the 1980s after a short-lived domestic flying career. (NASA)

risky investment. Therefore, one airline after another, which had placed (non-binding) orders for the Concorde, cancelled them and instead ordered the Jumbo. As it turned out, only 14 Concordes would enter commercial service, whereas Boeing sold more than 1,500 Jumbos over the next five decades. However, the Anglo-French Concorde, a

A house façade painted on the hangar wall makes it clear that the overall height of the Jumbo resembles that of a seven-storey building. (Pan Am Historical Foundation)

Pat Nixon, First Lady of the United States, christens Pan Am's first Boeing 747 the Clipper Young America in the presence of Pan Am Chairman Najeeb Halaby on January 15, 1970. Instead of champagne, Mrs Nixon sprayed red, white and blue water on the aircraft. (White House Photo Office/WHPO 2749-18)

Left: *Thanks to its enormous dimensions, the Boeing 747 was nicknamed the Jumbo. This term goes back to a very large male elephant that was brought to Europe from Africa in 1865 and sold to the U.S. after stays in zoos in Paris and London. Jumbo died in 1885 after colliding with a locomotive in the U.S.. The name of this extraordinary animal is still synonymous with greatness worldwide. (Duette Photographers/ Tufts University Collections and Archives)*

unique symbiosis of speed, high tech, and elegance was to become an aviation legend in her own right, and flew until 2003. Moreover, the Concorde programme proved the ability of European countries to work together, thus laying the foundation for the aircraft manufacturer Airbus, Boeing's future rival on the world market.

Watch Video: Pan Am 747

Although the Jumbo's future looked promising, its programme briefly

FIRST COMMERCIAL PASSENGER FLIGHT of BOEING 747
PAN AMERICAN WORLD AIRWAYS · JANUARY 21,1970
NO SMOKING BEYOND THIS PO

After several hours' delay, boarding begins after midnight to January 22 for the inaugural flight of Pan Am's Clipper Victor from New York to London. (Boeing)

stumbled again, when one of the five test aircraft was damaged during a landing attempt at Renton Municipal Airport, adjacent to the Boeing Renton factory, Washington. On December 13, 1969, a 747 test aircraft flown by pilot Ralph C. Cokely undershot the airport's short runway, tearing off the right outer landing gear and damaging two engine nacelles. However, nobody was injured. After 1,013 test flights totalling 1,449 flight hours, the 747 received its FAA airworthiness certificate in December of 1969, clearing it for introduction into service.

The huge cost of developing the Jumbo and building the Everett factory meant that Boeing, during the final months before delivery of the first aircraft, had to repeatedly request additional funding to complete the project. Had this been refused, the company's survival would have been threatened by the debt of more than $2 billion. Boeing president Bill Allen later said, "It was really too large a project for us." Ultimately, the risky undertaking succeeded, and Boeing held a monopoly in the production of very large widebody passenger aircraft for many years.

Entry into Service: The Age of the Jumbo

On January 15, 1970, Mrs Pat Nixon, First Lady of the United States, ushered in the age of the Jumbo, when she christened the first Boeing 747 at Dulles International Airport, near Washington, D.C., which was to see service with its launch customer Pan Am.

During the next few days, Pan Am flew several 747s to major U.S. airports as a public relations effort, allowing visitors to tour the brand-new jets. The airline began its final preparations for the first 747 service on the evening of January 21, 1970, when *Clipper Young America* was scheduled to fly from New York's John F. Kennedy Airport to London-Heathrow. However, an engine problem delayed the inaugural flight's departure by several hours, necessitating the substitution of another 747, *Clipper Victor* (N736PA). It left New York at 1:52 a.m. EST, almost seven hours after the scheduled departure time. The pilot was 49-year-old Captain Robert M. Weeks, a veteran of 28 years with Pan Am who had logged more than 15,000 hours on Pan Am routes. His co-pilot was Captain John Noland and the flight engineer was August McKinney. After its inaugural commercial six-hour and 14-minute flight, the jet, carrying 332 passengers and 20 crew, touched down at London's Heathrow Airport at 8:06 a.m. EST, and was warmly greeted by airport staff and the press.

One of the passengers, Mrs Joe Tepera of Fort Worth, Texas, later told the press: "The flight was simply great. Flying in a beautiful plane like that was worth the delay. All the passengers were good humoured and when the plane finally took off, they applauded. They did the same when it landed. I personally

Pan Am was the launch customer for the Boeing 747, and many other airlines eventually acquired the aircraft as well and used it as their flagship. The 747 was able to overcome concerns that some airports would not be able to accommodate an airliner of that size. (U.S. National Archives)

would not hesitate flying in a jumbo again." Michael J. Flynn of Chicago added: "The delay didn't bother me much. We were given a first-class meal. It's a good plane."[16]

After its introduction into service with various international airlines, the 747 initially suffered from a number of teething problems. The launch customer Pan Am, for example, had to contend with problems with the engine suspension and a performance profile that fell short of the manufacturer's promises. However, these faults were quickly rectified.

Passengers soon found the Jumbo spacious, comfortable, and affordable, as historian Michael Lombardi puts it in a nutshell: "The combination of the 747's size, range, efficiency of its design, and the high-bypass engines made it less costly to operate and less cost per passenger allowing for lower fares. [This] made it economically possible for anyone to fly and the range of the 747 greatly expanded the number of air routes – especially across the Pacific These factors greatly increased the numbers of passengers. Also, the unique first-class experience on board the 747 made it the first choice for business travellers."[17]

When asked what his favourite seat aboard the Jumbo was, Joe Sutter replied: "Row 3A, left-hand side of the First Class. You can get up there; it's quiet, away from everything. If you want to read a book, you can. If you want to get up and roam around, you can. Man, that's the way to fly."[18]

After entering service with Pan Am, other airlines that had purchased the jet to stay competitive in the contested industry began to put their own Jumbos into operation. While the new widebody jet enjoyed the lowest potential operating cost per seat, this advantage could only be achieved when it was fully loaded as costs per seat increased exponentially as occupancy declined. A moderately loaded Jumbo, with only 70 per cent of its seats occupied, used more than 95 per cent of the fuel needed by a fully occupied Jumbo.

Nevertheless, many flag carriers bought the new aircraft for image reasons, as Michael Lombardi explains: "Of course, the 747 had captured the public's imagination – it was the largest commercial jet in the world – passengers wanted to fly the 747. It was

Handover of the first 747 to Lufthansa on March 9, 1970. (Lufthansa)

clearly a flagship for airlines. It was such a prestigious airplane that many airlines bought them just for that reason rather than any other economic or business consideration."[19]

The recession of 1969/70 did not bypass Boeing. The 747 was not cheap. Each aircraft cost more than $2 million which is equivalent to about $157 million in today's value. For 18 months after September 1970 the company could only sell two Jumbos worldwide – both to the Irish flag airline Aer Lingus. For the next three years, not one American airline decided to acquire even a single 747. The 1973 oil crisis also led to higher fuel prices, which in turn resulted in higher ticket prices. These economic problems in the United States and other countries across the globe led to reduced passenger numbers. Several airlines concluded that they did not have enough passengers to operate Jumbos on a profit-making basis. Therefore, they replaced them with the smaller and recently introduced three-engined widebody jets, Lockheed L-1011 TriStar and McDonnell

Douglas DC-10, followed by the Boeing 767 and the Airbus A300/A310 twinjets.

Because of its enormous size, there was even some initial resistance to the 747, especially from some U.S. airlines, because there were concerns that most airports would not be able to accommodate the large jet. However, Boeing was convinced that all those airlines offering transatlantic flights such as the classic New York–London route and back would recognise and appreciate the advantages of such a large aircraft. An important factor was the fact that the Jumbo could carry up to 550 passengers – almost three times more than the 707.

Boeing needed the 747 to be successful, for the sake of the company, so engineers continued to tweak the design and listened carefully to customer suggestions and criticisms. As a result, various versions emerged in the years that followed, proving the versatility and longevity of the 747.

Watch Video:
On Board

DESIGN OF A MARVEL

Bigger, better, beautiful – the Jumbo not only embodies many superlatives, but also stands for highly developed technology. Since its maiden flight in 1969, it has not only set standards, but has also played a significant role in shaping the progress of aviation in many areas.

(John Powell)

CHAPTER 2

The Design

During the concept phase of the 747 in the 1960s, Joe Sutter's team produced several conceptual designs for an airframe that could carry more than the 350 passengers desired by Juan Trippe. One of these designs was also based in part on the proposal of the head of Pan Am. It included a full-length, double-deck fuselage with eight-across seating and two aisles on the lower deck, and seven-across seating and two aisles on the upper deck. However, concern over evacuation routes and limited cargo-carrying capability caused this idea to be cancelled in 1966 in favour of a wider single-deck design. The cockpit was, therefore, placed on a shortened upper deck so that a freight-loading nose door could be included in the nose cone, thus giving the Jumbo its distinctive 'hump'. The 747 was designed with a new methodology known as 'fault tree analysis', which allowed the effects of a failure of a single part to be studied to determine its impact on other systems. To address concerns about safety and flyability, the design of the giant and complex aircraft included structural redundancy, redundant hydraulic systems, quadruple main landing gear, and dual control surfaces.

The Fuselage

The fuselage is an all-metal half-shell construction with load-bearing outer skin rivetted to longitudinal and transverse frames. The passenger and cargo areas are designed as pressurised cabins. In the forward section, the passenger compartment consists of two decks, one above the other. The cockpit (flight deck) is also located on the upper deck, resulting in an unusually high seating position for the cockpit crew. Below the passenger area (main deck) is the multi-section cargo hold.

Stefan Hauke, Senior First Officer and Boeing 747 Deputy Technical Pilot (*Flottenreferent Technik*) at Lufthansa, praises the fuselage's construction: "The Boeing 747 differs from aircraft previously built or still in production by its sheer redundancy and airframe strength. When the 747 was originally designed it was 'all-hand designed', which means there were no computer programmes optimising the structure versus weight. It was all about

Although the Jumbo was constantly modernised, its external appearance remained virtually unchanged over the decades. (John Powell)

Assembly of the individual fuselage sections at the Everett plant. One after the other, the nose section, the centre section and finally the tail are brought into position with a crane and then joined together. (Boeing)

Aircraft overhaul (D-Check) on a 747-400 at Lufthansa Technik Hamburg. For this inspection, among other things, the entire interior is removed so that the complete aircraft structure can be examined. (Lufthansa/Udo Kröner)

the experience of the many designers, and because it was by this time (and for a long time to come) the biggest commercial airplane, Boeing designed it to last. For us in the technical department this is still noticeable as the B747's airframe is so tough and well designed that during all the D checks in its lifetime, we did not notice any problems with cracks and fatigue – unlike newer, computer-optimised airframes, which show problems with cracks in wings and fuselage as early as two years after entry into service. From a pilot's perspective it is a big and stable aircraft, which is still surprisingly responsive on the flight controls and a real pleasure to fly."

The D check, also known as a 'heavy maintenance visit' (HMV), is by far the most comprehensive and demanding aircraft check. This check occurs approximately every six to seven years. It is a check that more or less takes the entire aircraft apart for inspection and overhaul. Even the paint may need to be completely removed for a total inspection of the fuselage metal skin.

The Wings

During the Jumbo's development in the 1960s, Boeing engineers incorporated some of the most advanced high-lift devices used in the aviation industry to allow the massive jet to operate from existing airports.

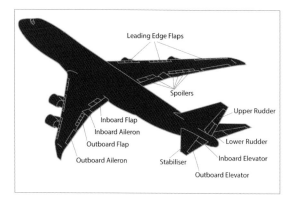

Flights controls of a Boeing 747-8. Extendable slats and landing flaps are used for safe slow flight during takeoff and landing.

To increase lift, the leading edge of each wing features three Krueger flaps (located inboard of the inboard engines) and an additional 11 leading-edge flaps outboard of the Krueger flaps. The trailing edge of each wing of the 747-100 through to the 747-400 (except for the 747SP) has one three-part outboard flap and one three-part inboard flap. The trailing edge of each wing of the 747-8 has one single-section outboard flap and one two-section inboard flap. These complex three-part flaps increase the wing area by 21 per cent and lift by 90 per cent when fully deployed, compared to their non-deployed configuration.

Six spoilers, which together are used as ground spoilers, speed brakes, and supplemental roll control about the longitudinal axis are arranged on each wing, of which the outer four are also used for (aerodynamic) roll support (turning around the longitudinal axis). After touchdown on the runway, they reduce lift and create more downforce on the landing gear.

Test pilot Mark Feuerstein points out an innovation: "The 747-400 introduced winglets to the type to reduce drag. The 747-8 changed the winglet feature to a raked wingtip, adding a small amount of length to the airplane's wingspan. Aerodynamically and structurally, the raked wingtip is more efficient. The 747-8 also used a supercritical airfoil design with a deeper cross-section enabling larger internal fuel wing tanks. The trailing-edge flaps on the 747-8 were also simplified using fewer flap sections than previous variants."

Like the wings, the tailplane is a self-supporting, all-metal construction with a standard design and a trimmable horizontal stabiliser. In some versions of the 747 – 747-100, 747-200, 747SP – weights made of depleted uranium were installed in the tail unit to suppress flutter. This led to numerous discussions, which is why these were replaced by tungsten from around 1981.

The Cockpit

Operation of the early Jumbo variants through to the 747-300 requires a flight engineer to monitor and operate aircraft systems in addition to the two pilots. Since

Top: *The left wing of a 747-300. There were no winglets at the wingtips yet; these only came with the subsequent 747-400. (Swissair/ETH-Bibliothek Zürich/LBS_SR04-001294/CC-BY-SA 4.0)*

Bottom: *The 747-400 received winglets to reduce drag. (Boeing)*

Left: *This photo clearly reveals the triple-slotted, or sectioned, inboard and outboard trailing-edge flaps. The pairs of fairings on each section of trailing-edge flap house the jack screws used to extend the individual flap sections. The picture also shows the landing gear in the extended position. The forward pair of wheels is considerably above the trailing pair of wheels on each outboard landing gear. Some of the leading-edge high-lift devices are also visible. (Adrian Arpingstone)*

Right: *The 747's wings incorporate the latest aerodynamic technologies to fly farther and more efficiently. The advanced airfoil provides improved overall performance and greater fuel capacity. (Boeing)*

This 747-400 is fully configured for a normal landing. Each of the main landing gear, two inboard body gear and two outboard wing gear, and the nose landing gear are extended. The triple-slotted inboard and outboard trailing-edge flaps are clearly visible. Less obvious are the 28 sections of leading-edge high-lift devices, 14 individual sections per side. Also visible on the underside of the forward fuselage, behind the nose landing gear, are the three triangular-shaped air inlets for the environmental control system air-conditioning packs. (Adrian Arpingstone)

Top Left: *The cockpit of the 747 is a sublime workplace (Boeing)*
Top Right: *In the 747-100, -200 and -300 Jumbo variants, the three-person cockpit with pilot, co-pilot and flight engineer was still standard. It was not until the introduction of the -400 that the position of the flight engineer was eliminated. (Lufthansa/Gerd Rebenich)*
Bottom Left: *The cockpit of a 747-200 has more than 900 switches, knobs and lights. (Swissair/ETH-Bibliothek Zürich/LBS_L1-726376/CC-BY-SA 4.0)*
Bottom Right: *The flight engineer was essential on the early models of the Boeing 747. (Swissair / ETH-Bibliothek Zürich / LBS_SR04-001989 / CC-BY-SA 4.0)*

the newer 747-400 and 747-8 have a largely automated glass cockpit, their operation only requires two pilots, though airlines typically have additional relief pilots on long-haul flights. Former Boeing test pilot Mark Feuerstein, who helped develop the 747-8, explains, "The 747 flight deck [cockpit] saw its most dramatic change with the 747-400 variant. A completely new crew-alerting and display system, pioneered on the 757/767 families, was introduced on the 747-400 in 1988, making the 747's flight deck a more efficient workspace. A new generation of engines and substantial advances in communications and navigation enabled the

airplane to be operated with two on-duty pilots at any given time."

In order to make the retraining period, or conversion from the 747-400 to the 747-8 short, simple, and therefore cost-effective, the cockpit of the 747-8 features only slight modifications compared to its proven predecessor, the 747-400, and also omits some innovations such as head-up displays (HUDs). Pilots with a valid type rating for the 747-400 can thus transfer to the 747-8 more quickly and do not need to obtain a significantly more expensive 747-8-specific type rating to do so. Depending on the applicable legal regulations of the country of

Co-pilot in the cockpit of a Lufthansa 747-400. (Lufthansa/Gerd Rebenich)

The 747-400 has digital primary displays and analogue standby instruments. (Bas Tolsma)

registration and the contracts of the pilots, a third pilot (and in many airlines even a fourth) also flies on long-haul flights of a specified duration or distance, so that one of the pilots can rest during the flight according to the rotation principle.

The Landing Gear

The Jumbo's massive landing gear is retractable and can be operated hydraulically and also 'freefall' without the aid of hydraulic power. The steerable nose gear consists of a twin wheel and is retracted forward. The main landing gear consists of four main beams with four wheels each. Two are located on the fuselage and can be used to steer under certain conditions, including up to a maximum deflection of 13° when the steering angle of the nose gear is 20° or more. This serves to reduce the turning radius.

The two landing gear linkages in the fuselage are retracted forward and the two linkages under the wings are retracted inward. Since the introduction of the 747-400, the wheels

Left: *Detailed view of the switches for the automatic flight control. (Bas Tolsma)*
Right: *The cockpit of the 747-8 features only slight modifications compared to its proven predecessor, the 747-400. (Boeing)*

of the main landing gear are equipped with carbon brake discs. These are controlled by a multi-channel, anti-lock braking system to prevent skidding during taxi, takeoff, or landing on wet surfaces. Previous Jumbo variants had used steel as the friction lining on the brakes. Mark Feuerstein elaborates on the safety of the design: "The landing gear system is an excellent example of the 747's dissimilar redundancy, which is just one of the aircraft's hallmarks. There are various dissimilar means of deploying or lowering the landing gear elements – there are five elements counting the nose gear – and not all of the elements need to be

The two massive main landing gears under the fuselage each have two axles with four wheels. (Swissair/ETH-Bibliothek Zürich/LBS_SR04-053931/CC-BY-SA 4.0)

properly deployed or lowered to execute a safe landing. Today, dissimilar redundancy is found throughout the aviation industry. But 747's architecture represents one of the earlier and most extensive applications of the principle."

The Hydraulic System

In modern aircraft such as the Jumbo, hydraulic power systems use fluids such as oil under pressure to drive machinery and power units or to move mechanical components. Redundancy, which is commonly used to ensure safety and reliability, is provided by independent hydraulic systems supplying hydraulic energy to various hydraulic components. The 747 has four engines and four independent hydraulic energy systems, each with various means of maintaining individual system pressure: engine-, air-, and electric-driven pumps are all used to pressurise individual systems.

Each of the four hydraulic power systems incorporates an engine-driven hydraulic pump and a demand pump, air driven on systems 1 and 4, and electric driven on systems 2 and 3. The engine-driven and demand pumps, the reservoir and their associated components are located at the aircraft's engine and nacelle area.

A demand pump is a hydraulic pump, which is only switched on during phases of high demand in the associated system. This could be due to actuation of a large

Top: *Two of the Jumbo's main landing gears are located under the fuselage and two under the wings. The nose landing gear is steerable. (John Powell)*

Bottom Left: *Close-up of one of the main landing gears. The 747 has a total of 18 tyres. (Bas Tolsma)*

Bottom Right: *Retracting the main landing gear during a test in the hangar. The aircraft is jacked up for this purpose. (Bas Tolsma)*

hydraulic-driven system, like landing gear or flaps. Another case would be if the engine-driven hydraulic pump fails, either the pump itself or the engine.

The engine-driven pumps on the 747-400 are also capable of operating at a reduced output with engine windmilling. On the 747-8 the windmilling capability of the engines is reduced, and so for the first time a ram air turbine (RAT) was introduced on the 747 to supply hydraulic pressure to system 3. An electric-driven auxiliary hydraulic pump in system 4 on the 744 and systems 1 and 4 on the 747-8 is used only for ground operations to

The four hydraulic systems supply not only the control surfaces on the wings, but also the elevators and rudders shown here. (Bas Tolsma)

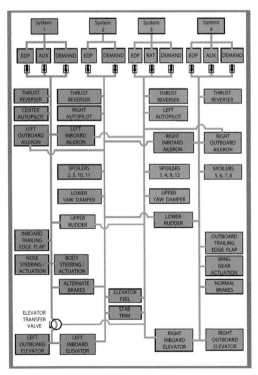

Schematic representation of the hydraulic system of the 747-8.

reduce the bleed air demand by the air-driven pumps during engine start. The four hydraulic systems provide power for the primary control surfaces (rudder, elevators, and ailerons) and secondary control surfaces (flaps, spoilers, slats, and speed brakes) on the wings and the tail used to control an aircraft's direction in flight.

Hydraulic power is also utilised for the operation of the landing gear system including braking and steering.

Air-driven hydraulic-demand pumps in systems 1 and 4 and electric-driven hydraulic-demand pumps in systems 2 and 3 operate to supplement the engine-driven pumps during periods of high demand. The demand pumps are capable of supplying the primary engine-driven system demands in the event of engine-driven pump failure. Air-driven pumps operate by bleed air from the pneumatic system; they can be supplied from engine or APU (auxiliary power unit) bleed air, or ground air sources. An APU is a device providing energy for functions other than propulsion. Each hydraulic system has an independent reservoir (not interconnected) capable of supplying fluid at all times.

Test pilot Mark Feuerstein points out: "The hydraulic system is another example of the dissimilar redundancy of the 747's systems architecture. Today, this type of dissimilar redundancy is found throughout the aviation industry. But the 747's architecture represents one of the earlier and most extensive applications of the principle."

The Fuel System

The 747-400 has eight fuel tanks, with a combined capacity of 57,164 gallons (216,389 litres) of Jet-A fuel. This amount has a weight in excess of 380,000 pounds (172,365 kilograms). The distribution of fuel among these tanks has a profound effect on how the large jet performs in flight. In particular, during a long trip, it is important to burn off the fuel in some tanks before using the fuel in other tanks – otherwise, the aircraft can become unbalanced. Although fuel management in the 747-400 is largely automated, there are still certain actions that are required from the crew. Mark Feuerstein goes into more detail about the horizontal stabiliser

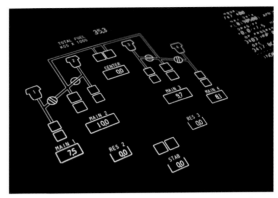

Digital display for the fuel levels of a 747-400. (Bas Tolsma)

Refuelling a Jumbo. The tanks of a 747-8 have a capacity of up to 238,604 litres. A 747-8 requires 3.5 litres on a route of 100 kilometres for each passenger carried. (Swissair/ETH-Bibliothek Zürich/LBS_SR04-050529/CC-BY-SA 4.0)

tank, the HST: "The 747-400 introduced fuel tanks in the horizontal stabiliser to enhance airplane range by maintaining the airplane's centre of gravity slightly farther aft during cruise flight. These tanks are filled on the ground and emptied into the centre wing tank during cruise flight. The 747-8, taking advantage of a thicker supercritical wing, introduced deeper wing fuel tanks with the same area as previous variants. The resulting greater tank volume, and the excellent fuel economy of the latest engine technology, yield superior airplane range."

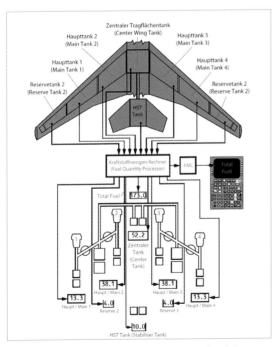

Schematic representation of the fuel supply of the 747-400.

Economic Aspects

The Jumbo can be placed in the market segment between the largest widebody aircraft with only one passenger deck, the Airbus A340-600HGW, as well as the Boeing 777-300ER, and the double-deck Airbus A380. In a typical three-class configuration, the Jumbo has a capacity of around 470 seats on the latest 747-8 model; it holds a monopoly position in this size range. Even during the 747-400's development, attention was paid to cost-effectiveness, which remains at a high level by comparison today. The new Boeing 747-8 model adopts some of the design features of the Boeing 787, resulting in a further significant increase in economic efficiency and environmental compatibility.

The Turbofan: Muscle Power for the Jumbo

To get the massive Jumbo off the ground and haul more than 350 passengers safely from one continent to another, it needed an entirely new engine – something far more powerful than the ones in use at the time.

"Propulsion development is hard," says experienced test pilot Mark Feuerstein. "It is often one of the pacing items of airplane development. While the propulsion path between the 747-100 and the 747-8 is not easy or straight, the engines powering today's 747-8 are very nearly carefree from a pilot's perspective."

Into play comes the JT9D turbofan, built by the American manufacturer Pratt & Whitney, an engine that would be a game-changer for civilian aircraft power. It was originally developed as a contender for the propulsion of the military transporter Lockheed C-5 Galaxy, but the production contract was eventually awarded for General Electric's TF39 turbofan.

However, this was not the end of the engine – the opposite was true. In 1966, Pratt & Whitney entered the 747 project because the company, Boeing, and Pan Am agreed that the existing JT9D engine had the potential to be developed into a commercial version to power the 747.

How a High-bypass Turbofan Works

When a jet engine is in operation, an incredible amount of air is forced through the rotating engine blades (the 'front fan') into the engine, of which a smaller portion flows into the engine core. In the core, the air is compressed, mixed with fuel, and ignited, thus driving the engine's turbine. That in turn spins the JT9D's huge front fan and propels the aircraft forward. Besides leading the air into the engine core, the JT9D directs a large portion of the airflow around, rather than through, the engine core, thus creating significantly more thrust for the amount of fuel it burns, creating a more powerful and more efficient engine. This made the JT9D one of the first 'high-bypass' turbofans to be used in widebody aircraft.

A Swissair 747-300 during takeoff. To allow such a heavy aircraft as the Jumbo to take off safely, the development of powerful and reliable engines was necessary. (Swissair/ ETH-Bibliothek Zürich/LBS_SR04-001231/CC-BY-SA 4.0)

Illustration of the JT9D turbofan from Pratt & Whitney. (U.S. National Archives)

Stefan Hauke, Boeing 747 Deputy Technical Pilot at Lufthansa, goes more into detail about the engine's operating principle: "A jet engine basically consists of a compressor, a combustion section, and a turbine. Modern engines have several compressor stages; each stage starts with a rotor (the turning part) and a stator (a fixed guide vane to feed the air into the next stage). The turbine also has several stages (here in different order) – always first a stator, followed by a turbine wheel. The turbine wheel is on the same shaft as the compressor, thus powering the compressor. The fan is just the very first stage of the compressor. It is called a fan, because it is not only a part of the compressor, it also moves the air around the engine, thus producing a large amount of thrust."

The bypass ratio (BPR) of a turbofan engine is the ratio between the mass flow rate of the bypass stream to the mass flow rate entering the engine core. For example, the JT9D's bypass ratio of 4.8:1 means that 4.8 kilograms of air pass through the bypass duct for every 1 kilogram of air passing through the core.

Senior First Officer Stefan Hauke (born near Dortmund, Germany, in 1979) has been flying for Lufthansa since 2004. After working as a First Officer on the Boeing 737-300 and -500, he first became an instructor, Maintenance Check Flight Pilot and Fleet Technical Officer for the Boeing 737 and later for the 747-400 and -8 models. Privately, Stefan Hauke enjoys flying and maintaining historic aircraft. (Stefan Hauke)

Every modern passenger jet uses high-bypass turbofan engines. When introduced in 1970, the JT9D was also quieter than existing jet engines of the time, creating a 'buzz' rather than a 'scream' during takeoff.

After ground testing of the JT9D in East Hartford, Connecticut, it made its first flight in June 1968 after being mounted on a Boeing B-52 as a flying testbed.

During the Boeing 747 test programme, Pratt & Whitney faced difficulties with the engine's design. Due to repeated failures during test flights, some 30 aircraft, unable to be delivered to customers, had to be parked outside the Everett factory with concrete blocks (instead of the engines) hanging from the pylons to keep the airframes balanced, awaiting redesigned engines. Boeing and Pratt & Whitney worked together to solve the problem. The trouble was traced to 'ovalisation', in which stresses during takeoff caused the engine casing to deform into an oval shape causing the high-pressure turbine blades to grind against the sides. The Pratt & Whitney engineers were eventually able to solve this problem by strengthening the engine casing and adding yoke-shaped thrust links.

The redesigned JT9D received its FAA certification in May 1969 and entered service in January 1970 on the Boeing 747. Over time, the engine also became the workhorse for the Boeing 767, the Airbus A300 and A310, and the McDonnell Douglas DC-10, with a total of more than 3,200 engines delivered.

Initially, the JT9D had a virtual monopoly position in this market. However, with the appearance of two competing products, the Rolls-Royce RB211 and the General Electric CF6 in the early 1970s, the market share was reduced considerably. Technical difficulties prompted Lufthansa, for example, to replace its first Boeing 747-100s with the JT9Ds early on with new 747-200s powered by General Electric's CF6s. Although Pratt & Whitney regained ground with the improved JT9D-7R4 version that appeared in 1982, the company never regained its lion's share of the early days. In 1990, production was

The JT9D was built using titanium alloys and nickel alloys. The engine featured a single-stage fan, a three-stage, low-pressure compressor, and an 11-stage high-pressure compressor coupled to a two-stage, high-pressure turbine and four-stage, low-pressure turbine. Advanced technologies in structures, aerodynamics, and materials allow improvements in fuel efficiency and reliability. (Swissair/ETH-Bibliothek Zürich/LBS_SR05-084054-24A/CC-BY-SA 4.0)

The JT9D-3 was the engine's earliest certified version. It had a weight of 8,608 pounds (3,905 kilograms) and produced 193 kN (43,500 lbf) thrust. This means that all four engines combined produced a thrust of 772 kN. By comparison, the four Pratt & Whitney JT3D engines in the Boeing 707-320C were only capable of generating a combined 340 kN. Over time, the original JT9D evolved into three distinct series. The JT9D-7 engine covers the 206-kN to 222-kN-thrust (46,300- to 50,000-lbf) range, and the JT9D-7Q series produces 236 kN (53,000 lbf) of thrust. Later variants, the JT9D-7R4 series (pictured here) cover the 214-kN to 249-kN-thrust (48,000- to 56,000-lbf) range. (Swissair/ETH-Bibliothek Zürich/LBS_SR05-084015A-18A/CC-BY-SA 4.0)

discontinued in favour of the improved successor Pratt & Whitney PW4000. A 249-kN (56,000-lbf) thrust version, the PW4056, was used to power the 747.

The Rolls-Royce RB211

Although Rolls-Royce, the renowned British aircraft engine manufacturer, had originally designed the RB211 turbofan for the trijet Lockheed L-1011, the company further developed the engine to provide greater thrust to power the larger Boeing 747.

The Rolls-Royce RB211 differed from other engines in its class (Pratt & Whitney's JT9D and General Electric's CF6) in having three shafts (triple-spool design) instead of two shafts. Each shaft has a compressor on its forward end and a turbine on its aft end. The RB211's three-shaft design allowed it to have fewer stages, thus giving it a shorter and stiffer structure. Moreover, it permitted each compressor to run nearer its optimum speed and efficiency, thus saving fuel. It also reduced the number of blades and other parts required in the engine. Although the three-shaft design had advantages, it was also (depending on the variant) up to 2,000 pounds (900 kilograms) heavier than the competing engines. (Glenn White)

By redesigning the engine, its thrust was increased from about 185 kN (41,600 lbf) to more than 220 kN (50,000 lbf). In 1973, Boeing agreed to offer the engine, now designated RB211-524, on the 747-200. British Airways, followed by other airlines, became the first customer to order this combination, which entered service in 1977. After Rolls-Royce had already unsuccessfully tried to sell the original RB211 to Boeing in the 1960s, the new RB211-524 boasted a notable increase in power, efficiency, and fuel economy compared to the Pratt & Whitney's JT9D that Boeing had originally selected to power the 747.

Like its American competitor, Rolls-Royce continued to develop the RB211-524, increasing its thrust through 229 kN (51,500 lbf) with the -524C, and then 240 kN (53,000 lbf) in the -524D, which was certificated in 1981. Notable customers included Qantas, Cathay Pacific, Cargolux, and South African Airways. When Boeing launched the heavier 747-400, this variant required more thrust. Rolls-Royce responded with the RB211-524G rated at 260 kN (58,000 lbf) of thrust, followed by the -524H with 270 kN (60,600 lbf) in 1990. The bypass ratio varied slightly depending on the variant. For the -524G and -524H, this value was 4.1:1. The latter was also offered as an engine choice for the Boeing 767. The RB211 was further developed into the larger engines of the Rolls-Royce Trent series, which are used, for example, on the Airbus A380.

The General Electric CF6

General Electric's CF6 turbofan is based on the military version TF39, the first high-power, high-bypass jet engine, which set a new standard in fuel efficiency. It was originally developed to power the U.S. Air Force's Lockheed C-5 Galaxy in the late 1960s. The initial civilian derivative, designated CF6-6, has a single-stage fan with one core booster stage, driven by a five-stage low-pressure turbine, which turbocharges a 16-stage high-pressure axial compressor driven by a two-stage high-pressure turbine. In 1975, Royal Dutch Airlines (KLM) became the first customer to order the Boeing 747 powered

The engine has a relatively high bypass ratio of 5.72:1. At maximum takeoff power, the CF6 develops 185 kN (41,500 lbf). The existing engine was further developed into the CF6-50 series, producing 227.41 to 240.79 kN of thrust (51,000 to 54,000 lbf). (U.S. National Archives)

by the CF6-50. A modified version, designated CF6-45, was also available with a 10 per cent thrust derate for the 747-SR, a short-range, high-cycle version operated by All Nippon Airways for domestic Japanese flights. Based on the CF6-50, General Electric developed the CF6-80 series (-80A, -80C2, -80E1) with a thrust range of 214 kN to 334 kN (48,000 to 75,000 lbf). The CF6-80 used on the B-747-400 produces 254 kN (57,160 lbf) of thrust and has a bypass ratio of about 5.1:1.

Besides the Jumbo, the various CF6s have also powered the Airbus A300, A310 and A330, Boeing 767, and McDonnell Douglas MD-11 and DC-10. In total, General Electric has delivered more than 8,000 CF6s and as well as some 3,000 industrial and marine derivatives.

The General Electric GEnx

Both the freight and passenger versions of the Boeing 747-8 are available exclusively with GEnx engines, adopted from the Boeing

787 and designated GEnx-2B-67. For this variant, the fan diameter has been reduced from 2.82 metres to 2.67 metres. The bypass ratio is 8.6:1. The engine, which was certified in August 2010, achieved significantly lower fuel consumption than the 747-400. But in order to achieve exactly the targeted 16 per cent reduction, the manufacturer developed, among other things, an initial performance improvement package (PIP), with which *the* engine-cell combination achieved the expected reduction in kerosene consumption.

To reduce the noise of jet-blast from the rear of the four wing-mounted engines, Boeing, General Electric, and NASA worked together to develop serrated (jagged) edges called 'chevrons' for the back of the nacelle and the engine exhaust nozzle. These chevrons reduce jet-blast noise by controlling the way the air mixes after passing through and around the engine. The acoustic liners and chevrons are

The mighty CF6 during an extensive inspection as part of testing at General Electric. (U.S. National Archives)

As the turboprops came on the scene, the reliability began to allow a reduction in the number of engines that, ultimately, people would be comfortable flying with.

"The first entries into the jet age, the Boeing 707, de Havilland Comet, and Douglas DC-8 needed four engines due to their increased mass, and to get people to trust them. These were mammoth aircraft compared to the piston-pounders that preceded them. The second-generation jets, the Boeing 727 and the 'Mighty Mouse' 737 broke a few of the rules. But then came the 747. It made all the others look like toys, and not only needed the four engines for performance but also for sellability (if engine manufacturers had today's technology in the 1960s, it could have been built with two engines).

such effective noise suppressors that several hundred pounds of sound insulation material may be eliminated from the fuselage, thus saving weight.

Four Engines vs. Two Engines

Captain Paul Jeeves became interested in aeroplanes at a very young age. He took his first flying lesson when just a teenager, and spent most of the following four decades as a pilot, including captaining the Boeing 747, the Airbus A330, and several other airliners.

Paul elaborates on the difference between four-engine and two-engine aircraft: "In the early days of aviation, next to the pilots, engines were the most unreliable beasts in the business. It was difficult to find any aircraft that carried more than just a few people built with less than four engines – the Douglas DC-4 and DC-6, the Lockheed Constellation, even the de Havilland Heron or Boeing Strato-Anything. This was especially true in the days when airlines flew piston-powered aircraft.

Captain Paul Jeeves holds ATPL licences in nine countries and has flown 38 types of aircraft. He has experience as a mechanic, a flight instructor, and a check pilot. Paul's other interests include sailing, writing and DIY projects. (Paul Jeeves)

Above: *As seen on this 747-8, the General Electric's GEnx engines feature 'chevrons'. These are the sawtooth patterns seen on the trailing edges of the jet engine nozzles. As hot air from the engine core mixes with cooler air blowing through the engine fan, the shaped edges serve to smooth the mixing, which reduces turbulence that creates noise. The noise emissions produced by the GEnx engine and airframe combination (total noise) are said to be 30 per cent lower compared to the 747-400 powered by older engines. (Lufthansa)*

Right: *The thrust controller for the four engines of the 747. If a single engine fails, only 25 per cent of the total propulsion power is lost and the jet can still be controlled relatively safely. If one engine fails in a two- or three-engine aircraft, more engine power is lost in relation to the total power. (Swissair/ETH-Bibliothek Zürich/LBS_SR04-001988/CC-BY-SA 4.0)*

"But, the four engines – even today – offer advantages over its two- (and three-) engine competitors. In two-engine aircraft, an engine failure at a 'critical' time can present some control challenges regardless of the pilot's experience and training. Before diving into this subject, the word 'critical' requires some

A 747 produces huge contrails with its four powerful engines. The contrails of aircraft with three or two engines are less impressive. (Chris Wood)

definition. During any takeoff in a multi-engine aircraft, there is a time while accelerating down the runway where the aircraft is too slow to fly but too fast to stop. This is the point where if an engine failure occurs, things can get challenging. Before and after that moment, an engine failure is not very dramatic at all. Keeping in mind that when such failures occur, the pilots are contending with 'nearly' a 50 per cent thrust loss. On three-engine aircraft (Lockheed L-1011, McDonnell Douglas DC-10, and MD-11, and to some extent the

A three-engine aircraft like the DC-10 has less power reserves than a Boeing 747 in the event of an engine failure; the pilot then also has to deal with asymmetric thrust. (U.S. National Archives)

Boeing 727) the control challenges depend on whether the failed engine is the centre engine or one of the outboards. The loss of engine thrust can be approximately 33 per cent. On four-engine birds – for example, the Boeing 707 and 747, the Douglas DC-8, and the Airbus A340 and A380 – a single-engine failure at the most critical time during takeoff is not much drama at all. At the most, 25 per cent of the available thrust would be lost, but this is an extreme case as 100 per cent takeoff thrust is rarely used.

"However, things become entirely different in the extremely remote case of two engines failing at the same time – especially if they fail on the same side. Things then are quite … exciting! However, the 747 will fly in such a situation. This begs the question, 'Why build aircraft with fewer engines?' The simple answer is economics. Fewer engines mean fewer parts, which, as a byproduct of having

fewer parts, means better reliability. After all, if a part isn't installed, it can't fail. And, fewer engines mean less fuel consumption – providing of course that the engine can deliver the same lifting capacity with lesser fuel consumption. Today's engine manufacturers have accomplished precisely that.

But what about the safety factor? As engines became, and continue to become, more and more reliable, aircraft manufacturers have been able to sell the various aviation authorities such as the FAA and the JAA [Joint Aviation Authorities] on the idea of long-range twin-engine aircraft. The certification lingo for this is ETOPS, meaning Extended Twin-engine Operations Performance Specifications. A colloquial aviation backronym is 'Engines Turn or Passengers Swim'. A popular question on many 747 fan club forums is, 'Could the 747 be built with only two engines?' Certainly, it could. But it wouldn't really be a 747, would it?"

THE 747 COMMERCIAL AIRCRAFT FAMILY

The commercial aircraft version of the Jumbo owes its longevity and versatility to its various successful stages of development. Over the past five decades, in addition to six successive versions, various sub-variants have been created to meet the manifold customer requirements and thus always remain at the forefront of development.

CHAPTER 3

747-100: The Beginning of a Long Success Story

On January 22, 1970, Pan Am's *Clipper Victor* became the first 747-100 to complete a scheduled flight. This first variant had a spacious lounge with three windows on each side in the short hump behind the cockpit. In addition to the *City of Everett* prototype, Boeing built another 167 units of the 747-100. Propulsion consisted of four engines from the Pratt & Whitney JT9D's first production version, each weighing 8,608 lb (3,905 kg) and producing 193 kN (43,500 lbf) of thrust. No freighter version of this model was developed,

but many 747-100s were converted to freighters. In 1972, the unit cost per aircraft was $24 million ($146.7 million today).

747-100SR

There were a few versions of the 747-100 that were delivered in smaller numbers even into the 1980s. The most common was the SR (Short Range) with 29 built. This was created at the request of Japanese airlines with smaller tanks, increased payload and could carry between 455 and 550 passengers in economy class with particularly narrow seating. From 1973 on, the 747-100SR was used primarily on short-haul

A Lufthansa 747-100. By 1970, a year after its maiden flight, 13 airlines already had the Jumbo in their fleets. (Lufthansa)

A Boing-designed First Class. The cabins of the first Jumbos were characterised by the flashy colours of the 1970s and featured a spiral staircase leading from the main deck to the upper deck. (Boeing)

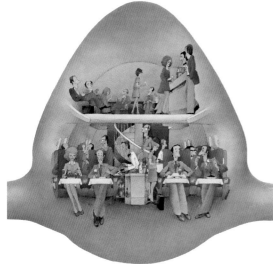

Advertisement for the First Class in the Air France Jumbo. (Air France Museum)

routes with extremely high load factors within Japan. The 747SR received modifications and reinforcements to the fuselage, wings, and landing gear to cope with the additional stress caused by the greater number of takeoffs and landings due to usage. Japan Airlines (JAL) ordered two 747-100B/SRs with an extended upper deck to accommodate 563 passengers. These jets were given the additional designation SUD (stretched upper deck). The engines were the modified JT9D-7A with 205.3 kN from Pratt & Whitney, or the CF6-45 with 202.8 kN power from General Electric. Further SR versions were built on the basis of the 747-100B (see below) and the later 747-300. The 747-100SR or 747-100B/SR remained in service until 2006.

747-100B

In 1979, the overall-improved 747-100B with a reinforced airframe and landing gear design was introduced based on the SR. This variant had an increased maximum takeoff weight of 340 tonnes (750,000 lb). Of the nine 747-100Bs built, the first went to Iran Air and the remaining eight to Saudia (now Saudi Arabian Airlines). Unlike the original 747-100, this

Initially, the upper deck in many Jumbos served as a luxurious passenger lounge. (Lufthansa)

After a short time, the lounge was supplemented or replaced by normal seating in order to generate more revenue per flight. Nevertheless, the lounge had contributed to the prestige of the Jumbo as a unique selling point in the 1970s. (Boeing)

variant was available with the modified Pratt & Whitney JT9D-7A and, for the first time, the General Electric CF6-50 or Rolls-Royce RB211-524. While Iran Air opted for the JT9D-7A, Saudia ordered its aircraft with the RB211-524. In 2014, Iran Air, the last commercial operator of the 747-100 and -100B, retired its last active 747-100B.

747-200: Another Milestone

A year and a half after the very first Jumbo's maiden flight, the second variant, designated the 747-200, also took to the skies for the first time, on October 11, 1970. The first airliners entered service the following year.

The main difference from its predecessor was its higher takeoff weight and greater fuel capacity. The resulting increased range made the Jumbo even more attractive to airlines, as it could now operate longer intercontinental flights.

In its first three years of production, the basic passenger version 747-200B was powered by Pratt & Whitney JT9D-7 engines, which were initially the only engines available. The range with a full load of up to 539 passengers started at over 5,000 nautical miles (9,300) and increased to 6,860 nautical miles (12,700 kilometres) with the introduction of more fuel-efficient engines. Most 747-200Bs featured an extended upper deck (the now famous hump), which could accommodate up to 16 passenger seats. While the first 18 aircraft delivered, like the 747-100, had only three windows on each side of the upper deck, all others were built with ten.

After the introduction into service with the JT9D-7 from Pratt & Whitney, Boeing also had the Jumbo certified with engines from General Electric's CF6-50 series starting in 1972 to increase the aircraft's market potential. Finally, in 1975, Rolls-Royce joined as the third engine manufacturer with its RB211 series when British Airways ordered its first four aircraft. The 747-200 was thus the first Jumbo variant for which customers could choose between engines from three major manufacturers. In 1976, the cost per aircraft was $39 million ($175.2 million today).

The 747-200 was produced in passenger (-200B), freighter (-200F), convertible (-200C), and combi (-200M) versions. Boeing built a total of 393 units of the 747-200 versions by the end of production in 1991, of which 225 were produced as -200Bs, 73 as -200Fs, 13 as -200Cs, 78 as -200Ms, and four as military or government aircraft. Iran Air retired the last passenger aircraft in May 2016, 36 years after its delivery. Today, only a handful of 747-200s remain in service as freighters. The last two 747-200Bs built went to the U.S. Air Force in 1990 and continue to serve the U.S. government today under the designation VC-25A. When the president uses one of these aircraft, it carries the famous *Air Force One* call sign.

747SP: Master of the Long Haul

Since the introduction of the Jumbo, Boeing explored various concepts with shortened and modified twin- and tri-engine 747

The Jumbo conquered the world with the 747-200. Characteristic features are the short upper deck and the ten windows on each side of the upper deck. There are five passenger doors on each side of the fuselage on the main deck and, from the 747-300 onwards, one on each side of the upper deck, with the doors on the upper deck serving exclusively as emergency exits. An exception is the shorter 747SP, which has only four doors on each fuselage side of the main deck and only one on one side of the upper deck. (Lufthansa)

variants. Ultimately, the company did not have an effective product in the long-haul and mid-capacity segments that could bridge the gap between the ageing 169-seat 707-300 and the much larger 380-seat 747-200B. New three-engine jets such as the Douglas DC-10 and the Lockheed L-1011 had carved out a niche that was costing Boeing potential customers. The main problem with any four-engine 747 derivative was overcoming the 33 per cent fuel-burn deficit it would have compared to a three-engine jet. Simply put, the more engines an aircraft has, the heavier it is, the more fuel it burns, and the more expensive it is to operate. Building a smaller Jumbo with more efficient engines and further modifications seemed more practical than a complete new design.

The go-ahead for the 14 metre (47 foot) shorter 747SP (Special Performance) also stems from a joint request from Pan Am and Iran Air. Both airlines wanted a widebody aircraft with sufficient range for long-haul routes from New York to the Middle/Far East (Pan Am), and for the planned Tehran–New York route (Iran Air).

Boeing decided to develop the SP as a four-engine aircraft (officially 747-100-SP) primarily based on the 747-100. Since it received the better engines of the larger and heavier 747-200 at a lower weight, it could achieve the same flight performance with lower fuel consumption. In addition, it required less lift

Business Class on board a Lufthansa 747-200 in 1982. Entertainment included a video projector that projected films onto a cabin wall. This technology was considered very advanced, as projectors with film reels had previously been in use. Later, several TV screens were installed under the cabin ceiling. Modern passenger jets are fitted with multi-function screens at every seat. (Lufthansa/Werner Krüger)

A passenger in a lie-flat seat in Swissair's First Class enjoys the music selection of the in-flight entertainment system via headphones. (Swissair/ETH-Bibliothek Zürich, LBS_ SR04-001453/CC BY-SA 4.0)

Compared to most earlier passenger jets, the Jumbo was given relatively spacious on-board toilets for passengers. (Swissair/ETH-Bibliothek Zürich, LBS_SR04-050446/CC BY-SA 4.0)

range performance than the full-size version of the day could manage. As Joe Sutter once explained to me, the 747SP also served to introduce the 747 to new customers, some of whom had originally declined the full-size 747 for fears that it was too much airplane for their respective airline. Joe further said that some of these airlines subsequently purchased the full-size airplane once they better understood how it could fit into their operations. Interestingly, the 747-8 [the final Jumbo variant] borrowed a design feature from the 747SP, the double-hinged lower rudder, increasing the lower rudder's yawing moment capability beyond that of other 747 variants."

The aircraft was powered either by Pratt & Whitney's JT9D-7 or Rolls-Royce's RB211-524. Between 1975 and 1982, Boeing built a total of 44 747SPs. In 1987, five years after actual production ceased, the company built one last 747SP for the government of the United Arab Emirates. It was delivered to the customer in 1989. In March 1976, a South African Airways 747SP with 50 passengers flew nonstop from Seattle to Cape Town. Covering a distance of 16,560 kilometres (8,942 nautical miles), this 747SP set the world record for the longest nonstop flight by a commercial airliner. This was broken in 1989 by the flight of an unladen

A 747SP from Pan Am. To avoid a loss of flight stability due to the shortened fuselage, the jet had an enlarged horizontal and vertical stabiliser. The 747SP's maiden flight took place in July 1975, and Pan Am and Iran Air took delivery of the first production aircraft the following year. South African Airways also used them on extreme long-haul routes. Among aviation enthusiasts, the nickname 'Short Plane' has come to be used in reference to the SP designation. Some 747SPs later served as government aircraft for various nations. (U.S. National Archives)

in low-speed flight and thus shorter runways than the heavier 747-100 and 747-200. For this reason, airlines that wanted to fly to large airports with short runways also ordered the SP. The overall weight reduction also allowed the installation of lighter one-piece landing flaps. Captain Mark Feuerstein served as chief test pilot for all Boeing 747 programmes for 11 years before retiring in 2018. He discusses the SP variant in more detail: "The 747SP had a rather short production run and was primarily used on routes demanding longer-

A Bahrain Royal Flight Boeing 747SP on takeoff from London Heathrow Airport with its landing gear retracted. The lightweight, one-piece landing flaps are clearly visible. The SP could accommodate 276 passengers in a three-class cabin, up to 331 in a two-class cabin (313 economy, 30 business) and a maximum of 400 passengers in a one-class. (Adrian Pingstone)

747-400 operated by Australia's Qantas. In 1977, to commemorate its 50th birthday, Pan Am organised Flight 50, a round-the-world flight from San Francisco to San Francisco, over the North Pole and the South Pole with stops in London, Cape Town, and Auckland. 747SP-21 *Clipper New Horizons* was the only one to go around the globe over the equator and the poles. The flight made it in 54 hours, 7 minutes, and 12 seconds, creating seven new world records certified by the World Air Sports Federation (FAI).

The 747SP production was discontinued because orders were below expectations, and in favour of the newly announced 747-400 because it was similarly economical to the SP despite its full Jumbo dimensions. However, the 747SP's takeoff taxi distance of 2,332 metres is shorter than the 747-400's

2,804 to 3,195 metres. The 747SP's landing taxi distance of 1,661 metres is also shorter than the 747-400's 1,920 metres. The 747SP can thus take off and land on much shorter runways than its successor. Today, only a few aircraft of this variant are still in active service, among other things as test aircraft for Pratt & Whitney engines.

A specially modified version of the 747SP is a research aircraft called SOFIA (Stratospheric Observatory for Infrared Astronomy). This serves as a flying observatory developed by NASA in conjunction with the German Aerospace Centre (DLR) for infrared astronomy.

747 Trijet (Unrealised Variant)

As part of the 747SP development, Boeing also considered a variant with only three

The 747-300 with the stretched upper deck was first delivered to Swissair in March 1983. This SUD has two emergency exit doors and is the most visible difference between the 747-300 and its predecessors. For comparison, a 747-200 with its shorter hump is under construction in the background. (Swissair/ETH-Bibliothek Zürich, LBS_SR05-200014-22 / CC BY-SA 4.0)

engines based on the shortened 747. This so-called trijet, designated 747-300, was to have two engines under the wings and the third, similar to the Lockheed L-1011, in the tail of the aircraft. Although Boeing had hoped to achieve weight and fuel savings with this three-engine design, the idea ultimately failed to materialise due to the costly redesign.

747-300: Intermediate Step with Extended Upper Deck

Introduced in 1983, the 747-300 represented a kind of intermediate step on the way from the 747-200 to the enormously successful 747-400. Compared with the 747-200, it was given a 23-foot- (7-metre-) longer upper deck. After the SUD (stretched upper deck) became standard on the 747-300, Boeing also offered it as a retrofit for older Jumbos and as a subsequent option for variants already under construction.

Minor aerodynamic changes allowed the 747-300 to reach a cruise speed of Mach 0.85 compared to Mach 0.84 for the -200 and -100 variants at the same takeoff weight. The aircraft was available with the same Pratt & Whitney and Rolls-Royce engines as the 747-200, but also with upgraded General Electric CF6-80C2B1 models. The combination of improved aerodynamics and more fuel-efficient engines made it possible to reduce fuel consumption by up to 25 per cent compared with previous Jumbo variants.

In June 1980, Swissair placed its first order for the 747-300. The variant revived the 747-300 designation, which had previously been used for an unrealised design study (trijet). Following the first flight in October 1982, the jet was delivered to Swissair in March 1983.

The unit cost was $83 million ($219.9 million today). In addition to the passenger variant, Boeing offered two other versions, the

The 747-300 introduced a new straight staircase with 14 steps to the upper deck, instead of the spiral one on earlier variants, making room for more seats above and below. (Swissair/ETH-Bibliothek Zürich, LBS_SR04-050617/CC BY-SA 4.0)

The extended upper deck (SUD) of a Swissair 747-300 in Business Class configuration. (Swissair/ETH-Bibliothek Zürich, LBS_SR04-001519/CC BY-SA 4.0)

-300M and -300SR. The 747-300M had cargo capacity in the rear of the main deck, similar to the -200M, but could carry more passengers because of the stretched upper deck. Like its predecessor, the 747-100SR, the 747-300SR was a short-haul, narrow-seat model for Japanese domestic service (including the Tokyo–Okinawa route). Depending on the version, it could carry more than 600 passengers, including up to 86 in the now larger upper deck. The last of the four 747-300SRs built flew until 2009.

Although Boeing did not build a freighter version of the 747-300, conversion of used 747-300 passenger aircraft to freighters began in 2000. The manufacturer delivered a total of 81 747-300s, including 56 passenger jets, 21 747-300Ms, and four 747-300SRs.

In 1985, just two years after the aircraft had entered service, Boeing announced its impending replacement by the more capable 747-400, which was under development. The last aircraft was delivered to Belgian airline Sabena in September 1990. While some customers continued to fly the 747-300, several major airlines gradually replaced

this variant with the 747-400, the last major operators including Air France, Air India, Pakistan International Airlines, and Qantas.

747-400: The Jumbo Becomes a Bestseller

Although the 747-300, introduced in the early 1980s, had a slightly larger passenger capacity than its predecessors due to its stretched upper deck, it did not feature an increase in range or a significantly modernised cockpit. At the same time, the jet's operating costs were steadily increasing due to a number of factors – most notably the use of a three-person cockpit crew (two pilots and a flight engineer), and relatively high fuel costs. Although combined sales of the 747-100, -200, -300, and 747SP models exceeded 700 during that period, the number of new orders steadily declined. The Jumbo, Boeing's flagship, needed a major upgrade. This was to be designated the 747-400.

Starting in 1982, the company introduced new engines, more advanced materials, and the so-called glass cockpit with a two-person crew on the 757 and 767 series twinjets. The

Right: The new 747-400's innovative glass cockpit included a Flight Management System (FMS) with large-format screens instead of the analogue 'clock style' still found on the previous variants. Heavy automation eliminated the flight engineer's work. For comparison (right): The cockpit of an older Jumbo with its analogue displays and the flight engineer's panel at right. (Lufthansa/Udo Kröner & Boeing)

latter eliminated the need for a flight engineer due to various automations, saving the cost of that crew member. The upgrade included new technologies, an improved interior, a 1,900-kilometre (1,000-nautical mile) range increase, more efficient engines and a 10 per cent reduction in operating costs.

The Jumbo's general seating capacity is over 366 with a 3–4–3 seat arrangement (a cross-section of 3 seats, an aisle, 4 seats, another aisle, and 3 seats) in Economy class, and a 2–3–2 layout in First Class on the main deck. However, each airline customer chooses a layout to meet their unique requirements. The upper deck, for example, has been used for all three traditional classes of service by different airlines, often in unusual configurations. (Glenn White)

Boeing test pilot Mark Feuerstein was enthusiastic about the new aircraft, saying, "The 747-400, which made its first flight in 1988, is probably the Jumbo variant that most of today's aircrews and passengers have in mind when they think of the 747. A longtime chief pilot for an Asia-Pacific airline described his first encounter with the 747-400 as stepping onto a spaceship. From a pilot's point of view, this statement was well founded. A completely new crew annunciation and display system, which had already been successfully pioneered on the 757 and 767 jets, now found its way into the 747-400, making its flight deck a more efficient place to work. A new generation of engines, along with significant advances in communications and navigation technology, enabled the aircraft to dominate long-haul Pacific routes for another decade."

The 747-400 received redesigned, longer wings with winglets and additional tanks to increase its range. In addition to the classic passenger variant, Boeing built the -400F freighter, the -400M combi variant, the -400D short-haul version (without winglets) for Japanese domestic service, and the -400ER with increased takeoff weight and range, of which only six were built, for Qantas. In 1989, Northwest Airlines became the first operator

The 747-400 received 6-foot (1.8-metre) winglets on its wingtips for the first time. Winglets, in all their various forms, are intended to reduce drag. Although the wings have an increased wingspan compared to earlier Jumbos, Boeing was able to reduce their overall weight by using composite materials and aluminium alloys. A 747-400 consists of millions of individual parts manufactured in more than 30 different countries. (Gabor Hajdufi)

First Class on the upper deck of Lufthansa's 747-400. (Lufthansa/Udo Kröner)

Business Class in the nose section (main deck) of a Delta Airlines 747-400. (Glenn White)

of the 747-400 with an order for ten aircraft. Cathay Pacific, KLM, Lufthansa, Singapore Airlines, and British Airways ordered the new jet a few months later, followed by United Airlines, Air France, and Japan Airlines.

The 747-400 was introduced with a choice of improved turbofan engines – the Pratt & Whitney PW4000 (replacing the JT9D), the General Electric CF6-80C2, or the Rolls-Royce RB211-524G/H. With a maximum takeoff weight of 397 tonnes (875,000 lb), the aircraft seats 416 passengers in three-class seating as standard and has a range of 13,490 kilometres (7,285 nautical miles).

In some configurations, the 747-400's range is sufficient to fly nonstop from New York to Hong Kong, which is one-third of the distance around the world. In 1989, a Qantas Airways 747-400 set a long-range record when it flew nonstop from London to Sydney, Australia. Although the jet covered the distance of 18,000 kilometres (11,190 miles or 9,720 nautical miles) in 20 hours and nine minutes, it was a delivery or test flight using special fuel with no commercial passengers or cargo on board. This record has since been beaten by a Boeing 777 and the Airbus A340 (for four-engine aircraft).

With 694 delivered to customers between 1989 and 2009, the 747-400 became the bestselling Jumbo variant. In 2011, they were replaced by the lengthened and again improved Boeing 747-8. In the late 2010s, and not least due to the slump in global air traffic as a result of the Coronavirus crisis, many airlines, for economic reasons, retired their older 747-400 passenger aircraft in favour of medium twin-engine long-haul aircraft such as Boeing's 777 and 787, and the Airbus A350. Production of the 747-400 passenger version officially ended in March 2007.

747-8: Culmination of Development

The attributes 'larger', 'quieter,' and 'more fuel-efficient' sum up the 747-8's progress over the 747-400. Mark Feuerstein, who was involved in its development as chief test pilot, sums up the progress: "In a word, the 747-8 could be described by *efficiency*. With an aerodynamically different wing, efficient structure, new engines, and improved systems, most operational metrics saw considerable improvement over the 747-400 – all while retaining existing access to airports, runways, and gates used by previous marks of the 747. It carries more payload farther with less fuel burn and considerably less noise, seamlessly complementing airline operational patterns built around the 747-400. The 747-8 was a natural outcome of long-standing customer requests for a larger, more efficient 747. Several named designs were examined from the mid-1990s onward, including the 747-400ER with longer range which was built in relatively small numbers from 2002. By 2005, anticipated economic retirements of 747-400F freighters, and to a lesser extent 747-400 passenger models, created an opportunity to launch the 747-8, first as a freighter. Traditionally, freighter variants of new models followed passenger variants. Launching the airplane as a freighter reflected a changing marketplace and the ever-increasing importance of air cargo. From programme inception, approximately three-fourths of future sales were expected to be freighters. For the first time, the first variant of a new model would be a freighter, not a passenger model. In some ways it is fitting closure to the original design assumptions made in 1966."

The slightly modified cockpit is based on the cockpit of the 747-400 to enable pilots of this type to retrain for the new version in only two days (thus saving time and money). No separate type rating is required for these measures. A significant technological innovation is the General Electric GEnx engines adopted from the Boeing 787, which should enable fuel consumption to be reduced by 16 per cent compared with the 747-400. In addition, noise emissions are also said to be 30 per cent lower. Because Boeing has an exclusive contract with General Electric, the 747-8 is not available with engines from other manufacturers.

Watch Video:
747-8 First Flight

The 747-8 Intercontinental takes off from Paine Field, Everett, for its maiden flight on March 20, 2011, before several thousand employees, customers and suppliers. The jet landed four hours and 25 minutes later at Boeing Field in Seattle. (Boeing)

Similar to the development of the original Jumbo in the 1960s, the creation of the 747-8 also stems from the suggestion of a long-time Boeing customer. Mark Feuerstein remembers: "As launch customer for the 747-8 passenger version, the Intercontinental, Lufthansa played a key, and treasured, role. Lufthansa had been operating 747s since 1970 and knew which improvements would be most valuable. From the very beginning of Intercontinental development, and continuing after the first delivery in 2012, Lufthansa would influence the design in thousands of ways. A very simple but important example of Lufthansa's experience and input involved the flight deck –

Watch Video: 747-8 Factory

more specifically, a lavatory located within the secure flight deck zone for exclusive crew use. While a minority of previous 747 versions had a lavatory for flight deck crew use, it was not a common customer selection. Lufthansa understood the value of improved airplane security, improved crew health and well-being, reduced cabin crew workload, and reduced passenger distraction and inconvenience, all resulting from placement of a standard lavatory within the secure flight deck zone. Lufthansa's insightful design choice became standard equipment on all 747-8 Intercontinental airplanes."

On February 8, 2010, one day before the 40th anniversary of the *City of Everett*'s maiden flight, the 747-8F prototype took to the skies for the first time with Mark Feuerstein at the controls and fellow Boeing test pilot Captain

Lufthansa was the launch customer for the 747-8, which is 5.6 metres longer (76.4 metres instead of 70.8 metres) than its predecessor, the 747-400, and almost four metres longer than the overall larger Airbus A380. This makes it the world's longest passenger aircraft. Both the passenger and freighter variants received aerodynamically revised wings with modified tips (raked wingtips) to reduce drag. New lighter and more corrosion-resistant aluminium alloys are used in the fuselage and wings. (Lufthansa)

Tom Imrich serving as the First Officer: "The maiden flights of the 747-8, in the freighter variant and later in the passenger variant, were exciting milestones. As with any new airplane, thousands of people around the world had worked for many years to make the first flights possible. Given the enormous work leading up to the first flight, the team was confident and ready. Yet everyone was also filled with anticipation for the work we knew was in front of us. The weather proved to be the dominant factor. Summertime in the Pacific Northwest is matchless. But the 747-8's first flights, both of them, were in the wintertime. The freighter's first flight was delayed several hours by fog. But the fog finally lifted to reveal a very still February day. From the first moment it was obvious that the 747-8 was in fact a 747 – easy to fly, sure, and graceful. Four hours later our test plan was complete and the real work began.

Captain Mark Feuerstein started flying in 1975 using money from his newspaper route to pay for lessons. Mark joined The Boeing Company following his retirement from the U.S. Navy and was the chief test pilot for all 747 programmes for 11 years before retiring in 2018. He is an Associate Fellow of the Society of Experimental Test Pilots and a Fellow of the Royal Aeronautical Society. (Captain Tom Imrich)

Top Left : *Lufthansa's 747-8 accommodates 364 passengers in a four-class configuration. First Class features Lufthansa's new First Class suite, now situated on the main deck and limited to eight passengers; Business Class features Lufthansa's new flatbed Business Class seat in 2–2–2 configuration on the main deck and 2–2 on the upper deck; Premium Economy and Economy class feature individual television monitors. (Boeing)*

Middle Left: *The newly designed staircase to the upper deck looks like a luxurious entrance hall. (Boeing)*

Bottom Left: *The new 747-8 is quieter, more fuel efficient and more environmentally friendly than its predecessors. General Electric's new GEnx engines, developed for the Boeing 787, are largely responsible for the reduced noise and fuel consumption. They can be recognised by their characteristic jagged ends. (Lufthansa)*

representing the hopes of a company that was still building the very factory from which the prototype emerged. By the time I was to fly the first flight of the 747-8, one day shy of the 40th anniversary of the *City of Everett*'s first flight, weather was still a problem, but the engines were largely carefree. But by now, 40 years later, the entire aviation world knew the 747 was easy to fly and many experienced 747 hands would be watching the flight live via the internet. The landing had better be reasonably good! Fortunately, it was. I would save my poor landings for another day."

747-X00SF/BCF

After the end of their careers, many old 747-100, -200, -300, and -400 passenger aircraft were converted to freighters. Since the early 1980s, these have generally carried the designation Special Freighter (SF) – originally, SF stood for strengthened floor. The conversion includes removal of the passenger seats, strengthening of the floor, installation of an automatic loading system for containers and pallets, and retrofitting with a large cargo hatch at the rear left of the fuselage. Unlike those aircraft built as freighters, the SFs do not have a nose door. There has also been a Special Freighter conversion programme for the 747-400 since 2004. The conversions are carried out by subcontractors in the People's Republic of

"When the *City of Everett* first flew in 1969, I was all of 10 years old and unaware of the event and that I would later meet several key members of the original 747 team. I didn't yet know that the first crew, Captain Jack Waddell, Co-pilot Brien Wygle, and Flight Engineer Jess Wallick, faced less than ideal weather, and less than ideal engines, all while

A Lufthansa Cargo 747-200. Since there are no passengers on board the all-cargo Jumbos, Boeing decided not to install windows. Thus, the freighters are easily distinguishable from the passenger variants. The exception is used passenger jets that have been converted to freighters. (Lufthansa/Werner Krüger)

The main cargo deck of a Jumbo is 184 feet (56 metres) long, about 20 feet (6 metres) wide and 12 feet (3.60 metres) high. The Wright Brothers could have made their famous first powered flight over the distance of 120 feet (35.5 metres) in the cargo deck or in the Economy Class of a 747. (Bas Tolsma)

China. Korean Air also has Boeing's approval to convert former 747-400 passenger jets into freighters for itself and other airlines. Aircraft converted by Boeing itself or by authorised partners bear the official designation 747-400BCF (Boeing Converted Freighter).

747 ASB (Advanced Short Body)

As a response to the Airbus A340 and the McDonnell Douglas MD-11 widebody airliners, Boeing designed a shorter Jumbo variant and named it 747 ASB (Advanced Short Body). Announced in 1986, this aircraft combined the advanced technology used on the 747-400, including the two-crew cockpit with the shortened 747SP fuselage. The ASB was designed to carry 295 passengers and had a range of 9,200 miles (15,000 kilometres). As airlines were not interested in this variant, it was cancelled in 1988 in favour of the two-engined Boeing 777 widebody airliner which became a success.

747-500

In 1986 Boeing carried out a study for a larger, ultra-long-haul version named the 747-500, which would enter service in the mid- to late 1990s. Capable of carrying up to 500 passengers, this Jumbo derivative would feature a stretched upper deck section, use more efficient General Electric unducted fan engines (propfans) and have a new wing to

Over the past five decades, the freighter variant of the 747 has established itself as an indispensable workhorse in world trade. The joy of this is written all over the 'face' of this 747-200. (Lufthansa)

reduce drag. With a faster cruising speed to reduce flight times, the 747-500's range of at least 10,000 miles (16,000 kilometres) would allow airlines to fly nonstop between London, England and Sydney, Australia. The 747-500 was not built as there was insufficient interest from airlines in relation to the expected development costs.

747-500X, -600X and -700X

In 1996/7, Boeing considered building two new 747 versions of different lengths in response to Airbus's A380, which was under development. The 747-500X and 747-600X were to have a wingspan of 253 feet (77 metres) and engines of the Engine Alliance GP 7176 and Rolls-Royce Trent 976 types, respectively. The fuselage length of the 747-500X was to be 250 feet (76 metres) and that of the 747-600X as long as 279 feet (85 metres). In a traditional three-class seating configuration, there would have been room for 462 and 548 passengers, respectively. In a single-class version, there would have been room for 700 and 850 passengers, respectively. The giant planes were to adopt some more modern systems from the Boeing 777, such as fly-by-wire controls. A third study concept, named the 747-700X, would have combined the wing of the 747-600X with a widened fuselage, allowing it to carry 650 passengers over the same range as a 747-400. Boeing was not able to attract enough interest to launch the aircraft.

747-400X, 747X and 747X Stretch

Between 1999 and 2001, Boeing again planned to develop two new 747 versions of different lengths in response to Airbus's A380. This was joined by a modified variant of the 747-400, designated the 747-400X, which ended up being the only version built in small numbers as the 747-400ER (Extended Range).

747-400XQLR

After the end of the 747X programme, Boeing continued to study potential improvements to the 747. One of them was the 747-400XQLR (Quiet Long Range) with an increased range of 9,200 miles (14,800 kilometres), higher efficiency, and reduced noise production. The improvements included raked wingtips similar to those used on the 767-400ER and engine nacelles with serrated edges (chevrons) for noise reduction. Although the 747-400XQLR did not go into production, many of its features found their way into the 747 Advanced, which was launched as the 747-8.

A Freighter for the World

The Jumbo's global and decades-long success story began as an underdog with sophisticated freighter genes. After an illustrious career as a widebody passenger jet, its production now ends as a freighter that has made and will continue to make its contribution to the development of international cargo air transport.

In 2018, aircraft carried more than 62 million tonnes of cargo globally. Although this represented only about 1 per cent of total global trade by weight, these goods represented about 35 per cent of all international trade. Because the Jumbo carried about half that amount for many years, it contributed more than any other aircraft to the rise of the air cargo business. Because of its development history, dating

To illustrate to the public the Jumbo's enormous cargo volume, launch customer Lufthansa drove 72 VW Beetles into the fuselage of a 747-200F under the eyes of its customers. (Lufthansa/Georg Wegemann)

back in part to Boeing's (unsuccessful) bid for a U.S. Air Force military transport, it was practically born with the talent to be a flying heavy-lift transporter. In addition, Joe Sutter and his team believed that the 747 would serve as a freighter in the long term, apart from a career (uncertain from the perspective of the time) as a passenger aircraft. Therefore, the Jumbo engineers, members of the famous 'Incredibles', repeatedly incorporated elements from the design of the failed military transport into the new aircraft.

In order to load the freighter version of the 747 as easily and quickly as possible, even with extremely bulky and long cargo, the aircraft was to have a large nose door. For this purpose, the cockpit was moved to a level above the main deck (cargo deck). This design feature resulted in the hump that is so characteristic of the Jumbo today. To improve aerodynamics, it was extended to the rear. The space thus created was used to accommodate a lounge in the passenger variant and later additional seating. Although the jet was designed to carry cargo in addition to passengers, Boeing did not initially offer a freighter of the first version, the 747-100.

Loading a 747 freighter through the nose door. In addition to standard containers, the jet can also accommodate special cargo items. (Air France Museum)

The 747-200M is a combi version that has a side cargo door on the main deck and can carry cargo in the rear of the main deck. A removable partition on the main deck separates the cargo area in the rear from the passengers in the front. This model can carry up to 238 passengers in a three-class configuration when cargo is carried on the main deck. The model is also known as the 747-200 Combi. As with the 747-100, a modified stretched upper deck (SUD) version was later offered. While KLM operated a total of ten converted 747-200s, UTA French Airlines also had two of these aircraft converted. (Lufthansa/Werner Krüger)

In 1974, a few 747-100s emerged with the capability to carry cargo on the main deck. These were former passenger jets of the Belgian airline Sabena. These jets received a side cargo door with access to the rear of the main deck as part of a subsequent modification. As a combi variant, they could thus carry cargo and passengers at the same time. In the meantime, Boeing had developed the second generation of the Jumbo, the 747-200. This variant also included an all-cargo 747-200F. After the first flight of the passenger version in October 1970, the freighter variant took to the skies for the first time on November 30, 1971.

The cargo capacity on the main deck of the first cargo Jumbo (747-200F) was impressive, with a usable volume of some 600 cubic metres, so it could accommodate up to 29 common standard pallets (125 × 96 inches or 317.5 × 244 cm). The freighters had a reinforced cabin floor and a cargo loading system in the floor, allowing quick placement of containers and pallets. Loading is done through the massive lift-up nose door. Optionally, a side door with a width of 11 feet (3.40 metres) and a height of almost 10 feet (3.04 metres) in the fuselage could be ordered. In addition to the cargo deck, there is also space for cargo in any one of three areas below the main cargo deck: the forward lower lobe, the aft lower lobe, and/or the bulk cargo space located aft of the aft lower lobe. While Boeing calls these spaces lower lobes, the airlines have many other names. There is room for nine more standard pallets there, so the 747-200F can hold a total of 38 of these pallets.

View from the main cargo deck of the 747 M (Combi) to the adjacent passenger area. (Swissair/ETH-Bibliothek Zürich, LBS_SR04-053766/CC BY-SA 4.0)

Loading a Porsche sports car through the side cargo door into a Swissair 747-300 Combi. (Swissair/ETH-Bibliothek Zürich, LBS_SR04-021758/CC BY-SA 4.0)

With a total of 73 delivered, the 747-200F proved to be a very successful cargo aircraft. Other versions followed over the next few years. In 1973, Boeing delivered the first 747-200C. The C stands for Convertible and means that the airline can convert its Jumbo from a passenger aircraft to a freighter with little effort. In addition, the combined carriage of cargo and passengers on the main deck is possible in five combinations. These aircraft generally have a nose door.

The 747-200M, on the other hand, which was introduced in 1975, could not be converted or modified. The M stands for Mixed and means that in this version the passengers sit in the front part of the aircraft, while the cargo is located behind it, which can be loaded and unloaded through a door in the side of the fuselage. With a total of 78 delivered, the 747-200M was also very popular with customers. Boeing also offered the mixed concept on the subsequent Jumbo variant as the 747-300M. Although there was no freighter version, the aircraft manufacturer started converting used passenger aircraft into freighters in 2000.

Success with the 747-400F

Following the introduction of the 747-400 in 1989, it took more than four years for launch customer Cargolux to take delivery of its first freighter (747-400F) in autumn 1993. By 2008, Boeing had delivered a total of 126 of the type. Unlike the passenger version, the freighter variant of the 747-400 does not have an extended hump. Basically, the aircraft consists of the fuselage of the older 747-200 and the wings of the 747-400, but various modifications allowed additional space to be created in the fuselage. The main deck (cargo deck), which is 184 feet (56 metres) long, about 20 feet (6 metres) wide, and 12 feet (3.60 metres) high, has a volume of 605 cubic metres and can accommodate 30 standard pallets. In addition, there are a further nine bays on the 130-cubic-metre lower deck, which alone is almost as large as the main cargo deck of a Boeing 737-800BCF.

For loading the main deck, the aircraft has a nose door and a side cargo door aft of the

The 747-400F has a maximum takeoff weight (MTOW) of 396,890 kilograms (875,000 pounds) and a maximum payload of 124,330 kilograms (274,100 pounds). It is easily distinguishable from the passenger variant by its shorter hump and lack of windows along the main deck. (Gabor Hajdufi)

Interior view of the cargo nose door of a 747F. On the main cargo deck visible here, numerous rollers and latches are built into the floor for moving and securing the cargo pallets. (Bas Tolsma)

Close-up of the very effective roller system on the main cargo deck of the 747 freighter. (Swissair/ETH-Bibliothek Zürich, LBS_SR04-002297/CC BY-SA 4.0)

wing. Using the nose door alone, objects considerably longer than ten metres can be loaded. The entire loading process takes about 90 minutes. The 747-400 also has a loading system: on the cargo deck floor there are rails between which numerous rollers are arranged that can be rotated by electric motors (power drive units). These move the containers and pallets along the rails into the cargo hold. In the door area there are rotating power drive units for changing the direction of the containers. On the main cargo deck and the cargo areas below (lobes), there are precisely defined slots marked by letter–digit combinations – for example, 9R, 9L, 10R, or 10L. Containers are usually loaded through the cargo door on the fuselage's side. The nose door is usually used for items too large for the side cargo door.

The containers are transported to the aircraft on dollies, small trailers towed by diesel or electrically powered tugs. After arriving at the Jumbo, the containers to be loaded are pulled from the dolly onto the platform truck, which stands right next to the aircraft and is equipped with electrically driven rollers.

The lifting platform truck then lifts the containers one by one to the level of the main deck and pushes them with the help of its rollers into the aircraft loading area, where

The 747-8 freighter on its maiden flight, February 8, 2010. It is capable of transporting its cargo to virtually anywhere in the world within 24 hours. Without efficient cargo aviation, modern world trade would be less efficient, as transoceanic transport is far more time-consuming. (Boeing)

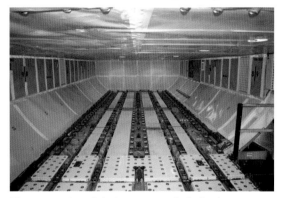

The rear section of the lower cargo deck. On the passenger and freighter variants of the 747, the lower cargo deck is virtually identical. (Bas Tolsma)

The standardised cargo containers are adapted to the shape of the 747's fuselage. (Swissair/ETH-Bibliothek Zürich, LBS_SR04-021833/CC BY-SA 4.0)

the power drive units in the floor continue to transport them. This is controlled by an operator at a control panel in the machine: he enters the desired position of the container or pallet in the fuselage, which the container then reaches by itself via the wheel and rail system in the fuselage. To prevent the load from slipping during flight, it is secured manually by holding devices embedded in the floor. Another loading system is used for loading and unloading the lower deck.

In addition to the pure freighter variant (F), the 747-400 could also be ordered as a mixed version. When Boeing engineers increased the jet's range by about 500 miles (800 kilometres), the company offered a freighter (747-400ERF) in addition to the passenger version (747-400ER). The freighter is the last variant in production. Atlas Air purchased the final four 747-8F aeroplanes, which are expected to be delivered in late 2022.

THE JUMBO
BEYOND AIRLINE
SERVICE

Since the 747's introduction as a very capable commercial airliner in 1970, the Boeing Company, the United States, foreign nations, and various organisations have adapted and converted some of its variants into government and military aircraft, transporters, and platforms for scientific research and experiments.

The Jumbo even proved that it could transport spaceships. The picture shows a model of the 747 with the space shuttle on its fuselage during wind tunnel testing. (Boeing)

CHAPTER 4

NASA's Shuttle Carrier Aircraft

Many people have called it the world's greatest piggyback ride – a space shuttle atop a Boeing 747. In the 35-year history of NASA's iconic spacecraft, millions of people saw both flying over cities, towns, and villages, generating tremendous excitement. But this was no ordinary 747: this was the Shuttle Carrier Aircraft (SCA). This specially modified Jumbo not only served as a taxi service for the shuttle, but also helped in the development of the shuttle itself. In its three decades of flying, the majestic image of a spacecraft joined to the SCA, became a symbol of American invention and ingenuity. Spectators would search the sky, and when they heard the roar of the engines getting closer, someone would shout, "There it is!"

Jeffrey L. Moultrie, a former SCA pilot, remembers: "It was always a pleasure to have the locals come out, to have the kids be able to look up and see a shuttle on top of the airplane. That's certainly a huge memory of mine. When I was a teenager in Huntsville, Alabama, … I

Watch Video: Shuttle Carrier Aircraft was looking up and seeing *this* airplane. How ironic that I would end up being a guy who flew the airplane and being lucky enough to be the last guy to fly this vehicle for the shuttle programme."

The unique image of two sleek vehicles attached in a seemingly impossible configuration, evoked feelings of progress, elegance, and achievement. To understand how the Shuttle Carrier Aircraft came to be, one has to understand the shuttle itself, America's first reusable spacecraft. At the end of a space mission, the shuttle would re-enter Earth's atmosphere, then it would glide down to a runway at the Kennedy Space Center (KSC) in Florida. There engineers would get to work refitting the spacecraft for its next mission. But NASA had other landing sites, such as Edwards Air Force Base in California. If the shuttle landed here, it would need a way back to its launch site in Florida. For flying the skies

on Earth, NASA engineers first thought to design the vehicle with its own jet engines. But these proved to be too heavy, too complex, and too costly to develop. Therefore, NASA would have to find another way to transport the shuttle.

John Kiker, an engineer at NASA's Johnson Space Center in Houston, Texas, remembers: "I made a little sketch of this and put it on my desk, and then after several weeks I called up Boeing one day and told them not to laugh but I wanted to show them something." Using model aircraft, Kiker and his team proved the concept of transporting the shuttle on the back of a Boeing 747. In addition, the tests showed the shuttle could be air-launched off the aircraft's back. The idea was accepted and the Shuttle Carrier Aircraft was born. The 747 prevailed over the Lockheed C-5 Galaxy due to its low-wing design in comparison to the C-5's high-wing design, and also because the U.S. Air Force would have retained ownership of the C-5, while NASA could purchase a Boeing 747-123 from American Airlines (registered as

For a photo on July 26, 1977, the SCA crew members pose in the yellow suits and the Enterprise crew in the blue suits. From left, they are SCA pilot-in-command Fitz Fulton, Enterprise pilot-in-command Gordon Fullerton, SCA flight engineer Vic Horton, Enterprise pilot (and Apollo 13 veteran) Fred Haise, SCA flight engineer Vincent Alvarez, and SCA co-pilot Tom McMurtry. (NASA)

Space shuttle Atlantis *returning to Kennedy Space Center after a ten-month refurbishment in 1998. Note the mountings that attach the shuttle to the SCA. (NASA/Carla Thomas)*

The SCA with the space shuttle taken from above during a ferry flight. This perspective conveys the difference in size between the two aircraft. (NASA/Jim Ross)

The space shuttle Enterprise separates from the shuttle carrier aircraft (NASA 905) to begin its first 'tailcone-off' unpowered flight over the desert and mountains of southern California. This fourth of a total of five piloted free flights took place on October 12, 1977. (NASA)

N905NA) in 1974 and own it outright. It was initially used for trailing-wake vortex research as part of a broader study by NASA's Dryden Flight Research Center at the Edwards Air Force Base, California, as well as shuttle tests involving a Lockheed F-104 Starfighter flying in close formation and simulating a release from the 747.

The SCA N905NA (SCA 905) first flew the shuttle in what was called the approach and landing tests, while still wearing the visible American cheatlines. The shuttle *Enterprise* was lifted on the SCA's back to an altitude of about 22,000 feet (6,700 metres) and air-launched. The aerodynamic tests were crucial in proving the shuttle's ability to glide down to a landing, and helped engineers refine the vehicle's complex design.

Just as significant, the imagery of the SCA and shuttle in action was the public's first glimpse of an amazing new era of spaceflight that was just on the horizon. The shuttle became a renowned and iconic space vehicle; the SCA allowed those NASA employees on Earth to share that excitement when it served as a shuttle taxi. As a result, mission by mission, SCA crews eagerly listened for word if the shuttle would have to land somewhere other than Florida. Jeffrey L. Moultrie explains: "We started getting excited when we heard the weather was bad in Florida. Those few of us flying this airplane liked bad weather in Florida as this gave us a chance to do our jobs. So as soon as we knew the shuttle was en route to California (and not en route to Florida), we started getting involved as the ferry team transporting the shuttle home to Florida. After their landing in California the shuttles were brought into the mate/demate facility and hoisted up, and the Shuttle Carrier Aircraft was moved under the shuttle and then the attachments were made for the flight home to Florida."

The precious shuttle could weigh up to 220,000 pounds (about 100 tonnes). To lift and fly with that much weight on its back, the SCA was specially modified, making it unlike any other jetliner. Most noticeable were vertical fins mounted on the tail. The vertical tip fins on the horizontal stabilisers improved the directional stability of the mated vehicle.

Other than the fins, there were additional crucial differences between a regular 747 and a Shuttle Carrier Aircraft. Inside the main cabin there was no insulation, no panelling, and all the lavatories and galleys had been removed to save weight. There were also

At the Shuttle Landing Facility at Kennedy Space Center, the shuttle carrier aircraft is positioned beneath the space shuttle in the mate–demate device (MDD). The MDD is a large gantry-like steel structure used to hoist a shuttle off the ground and position it onto the back of the SCA. (NASA)

The SCA lands with Endeavour at Edwards Air Force Base in California. (NASA)

two bulkheads providing support for the shuttle attach points. SCA Flight Engineer Henry Taylor explains: "The shuttle's attach points for the Shuttle Carrier Aircraft are in the same location that the shuttle attaches to the external tank for its launch into space. In the aft section of the SCA, there are two struts going up inside the shuttle attaching it to the SCA for the ferry flights. In the front, there's another small mount connecting the SCA with the shuttle's front section atop. Somebody made a kind of joke, although it's relevant: by the aft attach points it says, 'Attach orbiter [shuttle] here, note: black side down,' which of course, the black for the tiles ... it's a kind of a joke to make sure somebody doesn't put it [the shuttle] on upside down!"

In 1988 NASA procured a surplus Boeing 747-100SR-46 from Japan Airlines. Registered N911NA (SCA 911), it entered service with NASA in 1990 after undergoing modifications similar to N905NA (SCA 905). SCA 905 flew 70 of the 87 ferry missions during the operational phase of the shuttle programme, including 46 of the 54 post-mission ferry flights from Dryden (Edwards AFB, California) to KSC, Florida. After the end of the shuttle programme in 2011, it had one final mission: deliver the shuttles *Enterprise*, *Discovery*, and *Endeavour* to museums. Across the United States, for one last time, people got to see the unique vision of spacecraft and aircraft joined in flight. Upon its retirement in late 2012, it had flown 11,018 flight hours over 42 years, both as a commercial jetliner and as a NASA SCA, and had made 6,335 takeoffs and landings. Today, SCA 905 is on display at Space Center Houston with the mock-up shuttle *Independence* mounted on its back.

Upon its retirement in February of 2012, SCA 911 had amassed 33,004 flight hours over its 38-year flight career, including 386 flights as a NASA shuttle carrier aircraft, 66 of which were flights with a space shuttle mounted atop its fuselage. It flew 17 of the post-shuttle-landing ferry flights from Edwards AFB to KSC. NASA 911 is currently on public display at the Joe Davies Heritage Airpark in Palmdale, California, under a long-term loan agreement with NASA.

SOFIA: The Flying Observatory

A very special Boeing 747 known as SOFIA (Stratospheric Observatory for Infrared Astronomy) is a successful example of international collaboration as well as a successful large-scale research facility. A joint project between NASA and the German Aerospace Centre (DLR), it is currently the world's only flying infrared observatory. As such, it makes an important contribution to answering the many questions about the formation of stars, planets, and interstellar chemistry.

The managing director of the German SOFIA Institute (DSI) at the University of Stuttgart, Dr.-Ing. Thomas Keilig, explains: "SOFIA stands for a special kind of astronomy, namely infrared astronomy. In the visible spectrum, we mainly see stars and galaxies, planets, and moons. Stars are formed in dense clouds of dust and gas through which we cannot see. SOFIA offers the advantage of infrared radiation

Close-up of the telescope with the rigid door completely open. (NASA/Carla Thomas)

SOFIA is an airborne observatory built to study the universe in the infrared spectrum. It is also used to develop observational techniques, new instruments and train young scientists, science instructors, and teachers in the field of infrared astronomy. (NASA/Jim Ross)

because its long wavelength allows it to penetrate such dust clouds. However, these infrared wavelengths are absorbed by the water vapour in the Earth's atmosphere and therefore cannot be seen from the ground. Only above atmospheric weather, i.e., in the stratosphere from an altitude of nine to 12 kilometres, can this spectral range be observed by SOFIA."

The cockpit of the SOFIA jet dates back to the 1970s and requires a flight engineer in addition to the two pilots. (NASA)

Watch Video: SOFIA

The aircraft is a Boeing 747SP designed for extreme long-range flights. For use as SOFIA's flying base, however, it is not the jet's long-range capability that is critical, but its specific power surplus and its achievable service ceiling of 45,000 feet or 13,700 metres (FL450 flight level). Thus, SOFIA can climb to flight level FL370 (37,000 feet or 11,300 metres) immediately after takeoff, fully fuelled, and conduct astronomical observations there. Built in 1977, the jet was first delivered to Pan Am as a commercial airliner and then sold to United Airlines nine years later. NASA finally acquired it in 1997.

The converted cabin with the workstations for the scientists. During its ten-hour nightly flights, SOFIA observes celestial magnetic fields, star-forming regions, comets, nebulae, and the galactic centre. (NASA/Tom Tschida)

As Thomas Keilig explains, SOFIA is an 80/20 joint project between NASA and DLR: "In 1996, NASA awarded the contract for the development of the aircraft, operation of the observatory, and management of the U.S. portion of the project in the Universities Space Research Association (USRA). The German SOFIA Institute (DSI) at the University of Stuttgart has been fulfilling the German contribution to the project since 2004, which mainly includes provision of the telescope, but also assigning the German observation time. The United States and Germany share the costs in a ratio of 80 to 20. Similarly, 80 per cent of SOFIA observation time is awarded by the U.S., while 20 per cent of this valuable observation time is available to German scientists."

SOFIA has several German and American sophisticated instruments, which are used to investigate various astronomical questions. The instruments presented here weigh between 400 and 600 kilograms each and can only be flanged to the telescope individually.

German Receiver for Astronomy at Terahertz Frequencies (GREAT)

This high-resolution spectrometer, developed in Germany, is used for observations in the wavelength range between 60 and 240 μm. In this range, astronomers can precisely measure, among other things, the emission of singly ionised carbon (CII) at a wavelength of 158 μm. Such measurement results provide information, for example, about the gas velocities around a bright young star in the Orion Nebula and its influence on further stellar evolution around the star. GREAT also made it possible to detect the existence of special molecules in space for the first time, such as sulfur hydride (SH), deuterated hydroxyl (OD), and helium hydride (HeH+).

Field Imaging Far-Infrared Line Spectrometer (FIFI-LS)

This imaging spectrometer can simultaneously capture images and spectra in the mid-infrared wavelength range between 51 and 203 μm. For this purpose, it has two parallel channels from 51–120 μm and from 115–203 μm, respectively. This German-developed instrument is used to study the formation of massive young stars. In addition, FIFI-LS can determine the chemical composition and velocities of dust clouds of the interstellar medium in our own galaxy or in external galaxies on the basis of prominent fine-structure lines.

Focal Plane Imager (FPI+)

The FPI+ is a high-sensitivity camera developed in Germany for fast image sequences, primarily suitable for observing short-duration astronomical phenomena. On June 29, 2015, for example, SOFIA was able to position itself directly in the shadow of the dwarf planet Pluto, which migrated across the South Pacific during a two-minute stellar occultation. The light curve derived from the FPI+ data shows interesting details of Pluto's thin atmosphere, such as cloud layers and turbulence. These measurements had special significance because just 2 weeks later, on July 14, 2015, NASA's *New Horizons* spacecraft passed Pluto at a distance of only 7,770 miles (12,500 kilometres), transmitting a series of spectacular high-resolution images of Pluto and its atmosphere to Earth.

Faint Object InfraRed Camera for the SOFIA Telescope (FORCAST)

The American high-sensitivity imaging infrared camera FORCAST allows astronomers to study infrared radiation in a wavelength range from 4-40 μm. It can combine two channels with 14 different filters for imaging discrete wavelengths, depending on the chemical processes to be observed.

Echelon-Cross-Echelle Spectrograph (EXES)

One of SOFIA's greatest advantages is its ability to study molecules whose emission lines are blocked by the Earth's atmosphere. The high spectral resolution of the U.S.-developed EXES enables the examination of molecular hydrogen, water vapour, and methane from sources such as molecular clouds, protoplanetary disks, interstellar shocks, circumstellar disks, and planetary atmospheres.

High-resolution Airborne Wideband Camera Plus (HAWC+)

The American HAWC+ is currently the only active astronomical camera that captures images in the far-infrared range, enabling studies of the early stages of star and planet formation at low temperatures. HAWC+ also has a polarimeter to measure the orientation of incident light waves. This allows the mapping of magnetic fields in star-forming regions or even around distant galaxies. In the immediate vicinity of the supermassive black hole at the centre of our Milky Way, HAWC+ was able to show how the strength and direction of the magnetic fields there affect the velocity of rotating dust clouds.

In the first SOFIA project phase, measurements were made in a NASA wind tunnel to determine the optimal design of the aerodynamic fairing of the telescope aperture in the fuselage and, at the same time, to design the flow characteristics, so that the aircraft could be flown safely. Beginning in 1998, the conversion of the 747SP into the SOFIA aircraft took place at the American company Raytheon (later L-3 Communications Integrated Systems) in Waco, Texas. Before Boeing converted four used 747-400s into the 747 Dreamlifter starting in 2006, SOFIA was the world's largest civil aircraft modification. When looking at the exterior, this special jet can virtually only be identified by the large moveable rigid door. It is located outside the cylindrical fuselage cross-section and can be moved over from the left side of the fuselage to the right side of the fuselage in flight, thus allowing the telescope an unobstructed view into the sky.

The interior modifications, on the other hand, were much more extensive, as Thomas Keilig describes: "The structural fuselage cutout for the telescope covers a quarter

The SOFIA telescope as seen from the passenger cabin, which is located in front of the telescope. The original aircraft structure shows the usual green anti-corrosion paint. The new pressure bulkhead installed in SOFIA is the white 'wall' that now closes off the pressurised cabin to the rear. The telescope (painted in blue) is installed in the centre of the pressure bulkhead. Along the perimeter, you can see the black air springs for isolating the vibration. The telescope's beam of light passes through the black tube in the centre of the image. The yellow ring is the flange where the science instruments for SOFIA are attached to the telescope. (NASA/Tony Landis/OBS-0007)

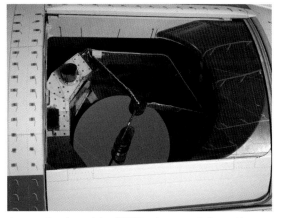

An exterior view of the SOFIA telescope. Reflected in the 2.7-metre-diameter primary mirror are the stars as well as a random aircraft flying by. In the centre of the primary mirror is the tilted plane tertiary mirror, which directs the telescope's beam of light to the left toward the detector in the cabin. Above, you can see the bottom edge of the rigid door on the fuselage's exterior, which closes the opening for the telescope. On the right is the aerodynamic fairing of the so-called aperture ramp, which prevents airflow from entering the telescope chamber and causing turbulence. Wool threads are taped around the telescope aperture with blue tape for aerodynamic studies during flight testing. (NASA/Tom Tschida)

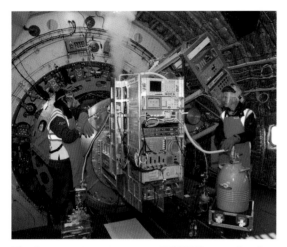

The German science instrument GREAT (German Receiver at Terahertz Frequencies) is prepared for an observation flight at the SOFIA telescope. Since the detectors only work at a temperature of 2 Kelvin (just 2°C above the absolute zero point), liquid cryogenic helium has to be replenished shortly before launch.
(NASA/Carla Thomas/OBS-0009)

Rendering of the entire SOFIA telescope, which has a total weight of 17 tonnes. (Deutsches SOFIA Institut)

of the fuselage monocoque construction and is six metres high as well as four metres long. The fuselage section between the still-existing cabin windows above the wing's trailing edge and the still-existing rear doors was completely rebuilt and structurally strengthened in order to redirect the structural loads of the empennage around the cutout in the fuselage. This required the removal of the doors behind the wings and the rear cargo door and the installation of a new pressure bulkhead. The pressurised

cabin was shortened by 30 per cent as a result of this modification. The new pressure bulkhead also supports the 17-tonne SOFIA telescope."

Because the installation of a 2.7-metre telescope on an aircraft had never been done before, this project presented the engineers with numerous complex challenges. To ensure that all the design changes really worked, they were first tested on a so-called mock-up before the modifications were carried out on the future SOFIA aircraft. The rear fuselage section of a decommissioned 747SP (serial number 21023/268) was used for the test setup, in which a new pressure bulkhead, a cutout for the telescope, and the door opening system were installed. A plywood model was also used to determine whether and how the telescope could later be fitted through the four-metre opening in order to be installed inside the SOFIA fuselage.

On April 26, 2007, the rebuilt and repainted SOFIA jet took off from Waco, Texas, for its maiden flight. On May 31, it was transferred to the NASA Dryden Flight Research Center (now Armstrong Flight Research Center) in California for further flight testing. Finally, on May 26, 2010, SOFIA saw its 'first light', which is the technical term for the first activation of an astronomical observatory.

The telescope consists of a Cassegrain optical mirror system with a Nasmyth deflection along the longitudinal axis of the aircraft forward into the interior of the pressurised aircraft cabin. First the beam of light is reflected at the 2.7-metre-diameter primary mirror and a secondary mirror, which is located at the very top, and then via the plane mirror (tertiary mirror), which is tilted in the centre to the science instrument's infrared detector. It works like any other telescope, but its uniqueness lies in the details. On the one hand, it is a lightweight compared to a ground-based telescope of the same size as it has to operate in an airborne aircraft. Nevertheless, the telescope system still adds 17 tonnes to the aircraft's weight. On the other hand, it is exposed to much harsher environmental conditions that require it to function just as well at –60°C in the stratosphere as at +50°C immediately before takeoff in the Mojave Desert.

Thomas Keilig elaborates on the special features of the optical marvel: "To prevent the aircraft structure's vibrations from being transmitted to the telescope, which would inevitably lead to blurred images, there is no rigid connection between the airframe and the telescope. The telescope, which weighs 17 tonnes, is mounted only on rubber pneumatic air springs, which keep all the oscillations and vibrations of the aircraft away from the sensitive optics. At the heart of the telescope's mounting is a spherical hydrostatic bearing, which allows the telescope to move on a thin film of oil around all axes with virtually no friction. This type of bearing is comparable to modern fountains, where a heavy stone ball can be rotated on a thin film of water. The telescope itself is inertially stabilised within this hydrostatic bearing, which means that the telescope is always precisely aligned in space with the observed target in the sky. Thus, during flight, the SOFIA aircraft moves around an immobile telescope that is rigidly fixed in space. The alignment accuracy that can be achieved in this process can be vividly explained as follows: A laser pointer aims at a tiny 1-cent coin located at a distance of 16 kilometres and does not lose sight of it for up to one hour. And it does so from an aircraft flying at 880 kph [550 mph] with the doors open."

While experts are now realizing the power and potential of this airborne observatory, SOFIA will certainly help rewrite some astrophysics textbooks. Thomas Keilig elaborates on some of the accomplishments that the German-American collaborators are proud of: "SOFIA's highlights so far include, for example, the detection of water on the surface of the Moon illuminated by the Sun in October of 2020, or studies of the different magnetic fields of very active starburst galaxies, such as M82, compared to spiral galaxies. The interaction of SOFIA's various instruments can be illustrated by the observations of the dust clouds rotating around the supermassive black hole at the

Dr.-Ing. Thomas Keilig studied aerospace engineering in Stuttgart. Since 2004, he has been working for the German SOFIA Institute (DSI) at the University of Stuttgart. At NASA in Palmdale, California, he was responsible for the airworthiness certification and commissioning of the SOFIA telescope from 2007 to 2011. Since 2012, he has been the managing director of the German SOFIA Institute. (Thomas Keilig)

centre of our Milky Way. First, these dust clouds, which do not glow in visible light, could be photographed for the first time with FORCAST in the infrared wavelength range. The FIFI-LS spectrometer was then used to determine the directions of rotation and the rotational velocities of these dust clouds. Most recently, HAWC+ demonstrated that the dust is forced onto these orbits by the black hole's magnetic fields."

The Global SuperTanker

As we learn almost daily from the news, devastating wildfires are among the most common forms of natural disaster in the world, including California, Australia, and Siberia. In addition to firefighters on the ground, who often risk their lives to save human lives, livestock, wildlife, and property by

The Global SuperTanker (T944) reigns supreme as the world's largest firefighting aircraft. Its capacity is nearly double that of the next closest very large air tanker (VLAT). T944 is the third firefighting aircraft converted from a Jumbo. The two predecessors were a 747-100 and a 747-200, and both are no longer active. (Steven Whitby)

extinguishing or containing fires, various aerial firefighting aircraft are also used around the world. The largest of these is a modified Boeing 747-400F, known as the Global SuperTanker and based at the Colorado Springs Airport, in the United States. This convenient location allows for quick deployment throughout the U.S., including areas with frequent forest fires, and provides the necessary infrastructure for the large and heavy aircraft.

Global Supertanker Services is a worldwide firefighting company specializing in providing very large air tanker (VLAT) services. The company is able to deploy anywhere in the world to fight fires, in addition to conducting oil-spill containment, and even pest control. With the ability to fly unrestricted in terms of airspeed and altitude due to the highly advanced integral tank system, the SuperTanker can be anywhere in the world to provide support within 20 hours of notification.

Watch Video: SuperTanker

David Allen, the vice-president of Maintenance, Materials, and Engineering, emphasises the strengths and unique features of the company's flying flagship: "Global SuperTanker is a force multiplier carrying up to 19,200 gallons [72,700 litres] of water or 19,200 gallons of fire retardant on a single flight. This provides fire managers options to utilise other smaller aircraft to focus on other fires, and fires where large loads may not be needed. Capacity is nearly double that of the next closest VLATs at 9,400 gallons [35,600 litres], and seven to eight times that of the standard LATs [large air tankers] at 3,000 gallons [11,400 litres]. SuperTanker's water/retardant capacity and flight endurance capability afford our customers an unmatched firefighting resource. More gallons per flight dropped, and a flight endurance more than any other air tanker in the world – that means lower cost, more time on-mission and fewer aircraft needed to fight fires. This improves safety margins and assists to reduce risk as fewer aircraft in the firefighting area means less exposure to ground and air crews."

Captain Marcos Valdez in the Global SuperTanker's cockpit. (Marcos Valdez)

Marcos Valdez is the Flight Standards Captain at Global Supertanker. He had wanted to be a pilot since his paternal grandfather first took him to an airport to watch aircraft land and take off, when he was around 3 years old. After flying the Douglas DC-9 and the Boeing 747-100/200 as a captain, Marcos upgraded to the Boeing 747-400 airliner as captain. He joined Global Supertanker in 2016.

Marcos describes the world's largest air tanker in more detail: "Our Global SuperTanker is a 747-400F that was originally built in 1992 as a passenger aircraft that served Japan Airlines for 17 years. In 2009, it was converted to a freighter under the BCF [Boeing Converted Freighter] programme and flew cargo until 2014. The following year, the aircraft was converted to an air tanker for the purpose of fighting wildland fires. Tanker 944 [T944] carries 19,200 gallons of liquid – water, retardant, water + foam, water + gel, etc – and delivers that liquid to the ground by using a pressurised system. The liquid is loaded onto the aircraft from the ground

at a tanker base, and the pressurised air for the delivery system is also uploaded from a ground-based air compressor.

"T944 is unique in the wildland firefighting air tanker world because of its capacity, its speed and its ability to fly as a normal 747 when en route to a fire and yet fly 'low and slow' to deliver the liquid to the fire front. When compared to other air tankers, we are just another tool in the toolbox. While T944 is the largest air tanker with the largest capacity of all the other air tankers, there are many roles that our aircraft cannot fill. Just as a small air tanker cannot make a three-mile-long drop in a single mission like T944 can, our T944 cannot fly deep into a canyon to drop 1,000 gallons of water directly on top of a specific tree like a helicopter with a bucket can do. All are tools in the toolbox and all are important to the overall success of the mission."

Marcos describes a SuperTanker working day: "As a crew member on T944, we wear many different hats and typically days vary greatly depending on what job we are doing at the time. In the off-season, we do a lot of meetings, public speaking, help maintain the jet, and ferry it to various maintenance facilities and trade shows.

"A typical day when actually doing fire duty is a bit more structured. We will generally arrive at the air tanker base 45

The giant air tanker carries 19,200 gallons (72,700 litres) or 172,800 pounds (78,528 kilograms) liquid (water, retardant, water + foam, water + gel, etc.). (Steven Whitby)

Dropping 19,200 gallons of fire retardant can be a daring task as pilot Marcos Valdez explains: "Flying air tankers comes with a very specific set of extra challenges. We operate at the lowest possible safe airspeed, and we do so very close to the ground. Flying this close to the edge as we do every day, it becomes normal to us." David Allen adds that, "aerial firefighting is not considered dangerous; it is, however, inherently hazardous. Many lessons have been learned over the years that have established rules, regulations, and limitations that must be strictly adhered to in order to ensure the safety of our team and the mission." (Steven Whitby)

minutes before the scheduled 'showtime' in order to preflight the jet and make sure we are ready to fight fires. We will then attend the tanker base morning briefing with all the other aerial firefighting crews and incident commanders. We will learn about the day's objectives, get a comprehensive weather briefing, tactical briefing, etc. We will then report back to the jet to stand by for launch orders. Some days we may sit *all day long* and never get a launch order, and other days we may fly five or more sorties fighting fires. It all just depends on the fire activity, the winds, the visibility, available lead planes, and other factors.

"Once we receive a launch order, things happen very fast! The ground crew will begin to load the jet with retardant. The flight crew will get a launch sheet with all the important information about the mission. This includes the location of the fire, the frequencies for four different radios (air command, ground command, helicopter command, and air-to-air), the name of the fire, other assists working the fire, and other relevant details.

"The crew will programme the navigation to get to the fire, arrange with air traffic control for any permissions needed to fly to that fire and prepare the jet for launch. The fuel company will arrive and upload

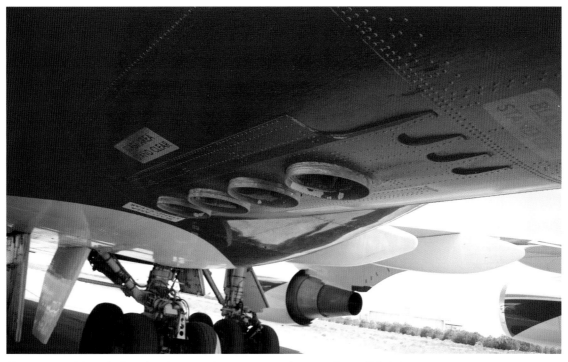

The crew can deliver the liquid to the ground via a pressurised system. (Steven Whitby)

the required fuel for the flight. We will then launch the jet to the fire. When we are 20 miles from the fire, we will contact our lead aircraft; that pilot will advise us of what to expect for the drop: single drop, split-load multiple drops, what the terrain will be, and what coverage level will be requested.

"The T944 drop system is designed to deliver the liquid in different types of coverage levels from CL 2 to CL 8. The coverage level is defined as a specific amount of liquid delivered to a 100-square-foot [9-square-metre] area, or 10 feet × 10 feet. A CL 2 is two gallons [7.57 litres] of water delivered to each 100-square-foot area. A CL 8 would be eight gallons [30.28 litres] of water delivered to each 100-square-foot area. We vary this delivery by choosing one, two, or all four of our drop tubes and by varying the air pressure we place on the liquid to force it out of the drop tubes.

"I have always said that when we fly T944, we are flying for the firemen on the ground. We work for *them*! My most memorable moments are

when we get to meet those firefighters and hear their stories of when a specific drop has helped them with their mission. We have had some very heartfelt moments with those firefighters. When T944 is called to duty in a foreign country, you must understand that they have already been on fire for long enough to know that they need outside help. When they call us, they are usually in big trouble. We are often told that when the Global SuperTanker arrives, we bring with us a symbol of hope, and a newfound energy to keep fighting the fire that has plagued them for many days, weeks, or even months. Meeting those people in foreign countries is an amazing feeling as a T944 crew member."

Civil Reserve Airlift Fleet C-19

The U.S. Air Force gave the designation 'C-19' to the 747-100s used by some U.S. airlines and modified for use in the Civil Reserve Airlift Fleet (CRAF), which is part of the United States' mobility resources. Selected aircraft from the country's airlines, contractually committed to the CRAF, support the U.S. Department of

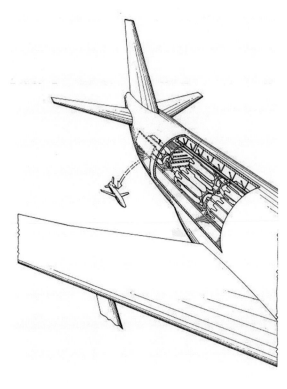

Left: *U.S. Troops disembark from a Civil Reserve Air Fleet (CRAF) Boeing 747 aircraft after arriving in Saudi Arabia in support of Operation* Desert Shield, *1990. (U.S. National Archives)*
Right: *Cutaway drawing of the CMCA's missile ejection system. (U.S. Air Force)*

Defense airlift requirements in emergencies when the need for airlift exceeds the capability or availability of military aircraft. CRAF has been activated as part of Operation *Desert Shield* (before the 1991 Gulf War) and as part of Operation *Iraqi Freedom* (2003 Iraq War).

747 CMCA: Cruise Missile Carrier Aircraft

During the 1980s, the U.S. Air Force considered replacing or complementing its shrinking fleet of costly B-52 Stratofortress bombers, many of which were retired and scrapped due to budget constraints, with a more affordable bomber. Boeing proposed to turn a 747 into a launcher capable of carrying more than 70 cruise missiles. The aim was to create a low-cost bomber, at 15 per cent the price of the Northrop Grumman

B-2 stealth bomber, but able to carry at least 50 more missiles than the B-52.

Named the Cruise Missile Carrier Aircraft (CMCA), a major benefit was that the enemy would find it difficult to separate a military Boeing 747 from a civilian 747 as it would have been flexible enough to land at civilian airports without raising alarm among nearby residents.

The CMCA design was based on the cargo variant 747-200C, with nine launchers mounted on tracks inside of the cabin and each launcher holding eight AGM-86 ALCM cruise missiles. An ejector system would push the missiles into the airstream from a door on the right side of the aircraft's tail cone. The area where First Class passengers would usually sit would instead house a command-and-control centre. This project did not leave the drawing boards as the U.S. Air Force abandoned it due to two factors: the Rockwell

In retrospect the CMCA, eventually upgraded with smaller GPS guided munitions, could probably have been an effective loitering weapons platform, capable of operating at much lower cost than the B-1 or B-52 bombers, orbiting high over Afghanistan and Iraq. The CMCA arsenal ship concept was ahead of its time in the 1980s as smart GPS-guided munitions were some 20 years from being fielded operationally. (U.S. Air Force)

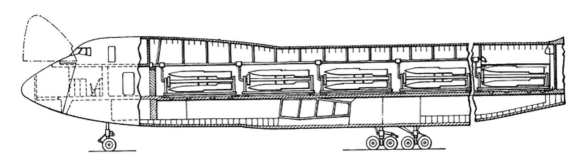

Side view cutaway drawing of the CMCA showing the arrangement of cruise missiles inside the fuselage. (U.S. Air Force)

B-1 bomber received more funding and the existing B-52 fleet received various upgrades under the Reagan administration.

Airborne Aircraft Carrier (AAC)

During the early 1970s, Boeing investigated the potential use of a 747-200 as an airborne aircraft carrier (AAC). This highly ambitious project took place under a contract from the U.S. Air Force Flight Dynamics Laboratory (USAF FDL) at Wright-Patterson Air Force Base,

Ohio. It envisioned an AAC capable not only of launching and retrieving several specially designed 'microfighters' (Boeing Model 985-121), but also refuelling them in flight and, on retrieval, rearming, and refuelling them for their next sortie. The idea included a complementary 747 airborne warning and control system (AWACS) version with reconnaissance aircraft. Boeing believed that this concept would be capable of delivering a flexible and fast carrier platform with global

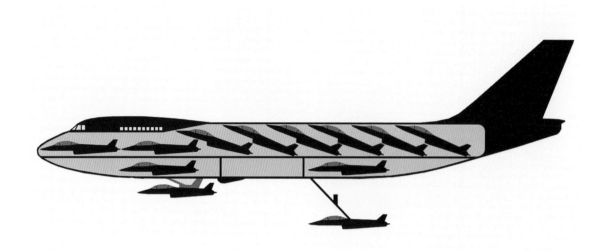

Cutaway drawing of the Airborne Aircraft Carrier (AAC). (U.S. Department of Defense)

reach, particularly where other U.S. or Allied bases were not available, or where seaborne aircraft carriers could not operate. Besides the 747-200, the Lockheed C-5A Galaxy was considered as the base aircraft for conversion into a flying aircraft carrier. Although this very ambitious concept was considered technically feasible, the AAC was never built due to the enormous development costs. The idea of an AAC is not new. During the 1930s, the U.S. Navy's helium-filled rigid airships *Akron* and *Macon* were regarded as potential "flying aircraft carriers," carrying four to five biplanes for reconnaissance.

Boeing C-33

During the mid-1990s, the U.S. Department of Defense engaged in a comprehensive process to refine airlift requirements, analyze various aspects of airlift, and investigate a potential airlift fleet mix. Therefore, a cost and operational effectiveness analysis was conducted to examine the potential augmentation of the existing McDonnell Douglas/Boeing C-17 Globemaster fleet with mixes of alternative aircraft, and to preserve intra-theatre airlift capacity. Additional aircraft candidates included modified Boeing

747-400Fs (renamed C-33), Lockheed-Martin C-5 Galaxys (restart of production line), and Lockheed C-141 Starlifters (extension of service life).

The 1994 NDAA study (Non-Developmental Airlift Aircraft) for the Boeing 747-400F called for various modifications including hardened decks, a flip-up nose and a ramp system for easy straight-in loading versus the commercial industry's side-mounted cargo-door-style loading.

The 747-400F's purchase and conversion costs were considered lower than the acquisition of the C-17. Although the 747 also had a longer range, it could not use austere runways or handle oversized military equipment in a way that the C-17 could. The 747's operating costs were also expected to be higher.

The U.S. Department of Defense finally came to the conclusion that the proposed airlift fleet mix, however, did not allow for a full strategic brigade airdrop nor was it optimised for tactical airlift requirements and lesser regional contingencies in support of peace-enforcement scenarios. Eventually, the plan to acquire the 747-400F (or any other type of aircraft) was cancelled in favour of purchasing additional C-17s.

Boeing E-4 Advanced Airborne Command Post

Watch Video: E-4B Nightwatch

The U.S. Air Force's Boeing E-4 Advanced Airborne Command Post (project name *Nightwatch*) was specially built to serve as the National Airborne Operations Center. It serves as a key component of the National Military Command System for the U.S. president, the secretary of defense and the Joint Chiefs of Staff (JCS). In case of war, national emergency, or destruction of ground command and control centres, the E-4 provides a highly survivable command, control, and communications centre. It is capable of directing U.S. forces, executing emergency war orders and coordinating actions by civil authorities. Outside the continental United States, the E-4 provides travel support for the secretary of defense and his staff to ensure command and control connectivity.

Two of the selected 747-200 airframes were originally built as commercial airliners. But when the customer did not complete the order in 1973, Boeing sold these two aircraft (powered by the Pratt & Whitney JT9D) and, a little later, a third one (powered by the General Electric F103) to the air force. After being modified and designated E-4A, they were delivered to Andrews AFB, Maryland, in 1974/5, replacing the Boeing EC-135 then in use. The F103 (based on the CF6) engine was later made standard and retrofitted to the previous two aircraft. The E-4A housed the same equipment as the previous EC-135, but offered more space and an ability to remain aloft longer.

An E-4B from Global Strike Command is refuelled by a Boeing C-135 Stratotanker from Travis Air Force Base, California., during a local mission on June 12, 2017. (U.S. Air Force/Staff Sgt. Nicole Leidholm)

Secretary of Defense Leon E. Panetta briefs the press on board an E-4B aircraft during a flight in 2012. (U.S. Dept. of Defense/Erin A. Kirk-Cuomo)

An E-4B flies over the Canadian Pacific coast in April 2014. During an endurance test flight, the jet remained airborne and fully operational for 35 hours. However, the E-4B was designed to remain airborne for a full week in the event of an emergency. It takes two fully loaded KC-135 tankers to fully refuel an E-4B. (U.S. Air Force/Senior Airman Mary O'Dell)

The pilots of the E-4B manoeuvre the jet into the right position for safe aerial refuelling. Like many older jets that have been upgraded with selected digital displays, the E-4B uses a mix of traditional analogue and modern digital instruments.
(U.S. Dept. of Defense/Army Sgt. Amber I. Smith)

In 1980, Boeing delivered the first E-4B to the air force, which offered a vast increase in communications capability over the previous model and was considered to be 'hardened' against the effects of electromagnetic pulse (EMP) from a nuclear blast. This meant that all equipment and wiring on board was shielded from EMP. Additional steps were taken to block radiation from the aircraft's cabin air management system and cockpit. By 1985 all three E-4As had been retrofitted to the E-4B model standard.

The four jets are capable of being refuelled in flight. The E-4B's main deck is divided into six functional areas: a command work area, conference room, briefing room, an operations team work area, communications area, and rest area. The jet offers seating for up to 112 people, including a joint-service operations team, air force flight crew, maintenance and

An E-4B aircraft sits on the tarmac at Travis Air Force Base, California. Note the large streamlined radome on the dorsal surface directly behind the upper deck. This contains the jet's SHF satellite antenna for global communication.
(U.S. Air Force/Louis Briscese)

An Iranian Air Force 747-100 air-refuelling tanker (tail number 5-8107) in formation flight with a MiG-29, a F-4E Phantom II and a F-14A Tomcat, simulating an in-flight refuelling. This 747 first flew on August 4, 1971. After delivery to Trans World Airlines (TWA) for commercial service, it was converted and sold to the Iranian Air Force in 1975. The aircraft is still operational as a tanker. (Shahram Sharif)

security component, communications team, and selected augmentees. The E-4B has the largest crew of any aircraft in the U.S. Air Force. It has an advanced satellite communications system providing worldwide communication for senior leaders through the airborne operations centre. To support these leaders without delay, at least one aircraft is always on a 24/7 alert.

The E-4B is also used by the Federal Emergency Management Agency, which provides communications and command centre capability to relief efforts following natural disasters, such as hurricanes and earthquakes. All E-4B aircraft are assigned to the 595th Command and Control Group at Offutt Air Force Base, Nebraska.

747-100 Tanker (KC-747)

The 747 heavy tanker-transport concept evolved out of a mid-1960s U.S. Air Force initiative to field a much larger tanker than the plentiful KC-135 Stratotanker, which was derived from the 707. This eventually resulted

in the Advanced Tanker-Cargo Aircraft programme (ATCA). By the mid-1970s, there were two finalists, the McDonnell Douglas DC-10 (as the KC-10) and the 747. The first 747 prototype, the *City of Everett*, was adapted to be tested as the KC-747, also known as the KC-25 in USAF parlance. Its boom configuration was very closely modelled on the tried and tested flying boom used on the KC-135. In subsequent testing with various receivers, including the SR-71 *Blackbird*, the KC-747 proved to be a stable and capable platform.

In its final production configuration, the aircraft would have had its own air refuelling receptacle on its nose, so that it could itself be refuelled in flight by another tanker.

The U.S. Air Force's E-4 Airborne Command Post, known as *Nightwatch*, which entered service around the same time the KC-25, was developed, and the VC-25A, known as the presidential *Air Force One*, were also based on the 747 and both had such an air-refuelling receptacle on the nose.

The KC-747 would also have featured a tilt-up nose for easy loading and unloading of large cargo, and there were even plans for a self-deployable ramp for rolling wheeled and tracked vehicles on and off the aircraft without the use of a lift. The KC-747 could haul more weight and volume, offer more fuel for supplying other aircraft (over 100,000 pounds more – a whole KC-135's worth) and had a greater endurance than the KC-10. However, the KC-10, known as the *Extender*, was cheaper to purchase and to operate, and could be used from shorter runways under certain weight configurations than the KC-747.

By 1977 the air force chose the KC-10 to fulfill its heavy tanker requirement. However, the whole KC-747 concept was not a total loss as three of these tankers, along with nine 747 freighters, were procured by Iran. At that time the Imperial Iranian Airforce (IIAF) had hundreds of American-built fighter jets on order and the KC-747 was the tanker aircraft of choice to refuel them in flight along with the existing less-capable KC-707 tankers. In fact, the IIAF planned to purchase many more KC-747s but the end of the Shah's reign in 1979 due to the Iranian Revolution prevented the delivery of additional aircraft.

During the Iran–Iraq War (1980–8), two 747 tankers were used for aerial refuelling, when Iranian F-4 Phantoms attacked airbases of the Iraqi Air Force at the H-3 Air Base in western Iraq. Destroying at least 48 aircraft on the ground with no losses of their own, this surprise attack is considered one of the most successful raids in modern aerial warfare.

The three KC-747 tankers are still in the inventory of the current IRIAF (Islamic Republic of Iran Air Force), one of which is currently operational. Some of the 747-200 freighters are also still in the fleet, of which two are currently active. Some of the jets are expected to return to service.

Boeing KC-33A

A proposed 747 was also adapted as an aerial refuelling tanker and was bid against the DC-10-30 during the 1970s Advanced Cargo Transport Aircraft (ACTA) programme that produced the KC-10A Extender. This aircraft is based upon existing Boeing 747 aircraft and combines midair refuelling capabilities with a reinforced upper deck that can carry vehicles, particularly light armour, such as the M113A3. A foldout ramp would be carried in the nose of the aircraft to allow vehicles to drive on and off of the aircraft. Under the deck would be a set of tanks and pumps to allow the aircraft to refuel other aircraft or simply engage in very long-range missions. The ACTA programme leaders finally chose the DC-10-30, which entered service as the KC-10A Extender. The main reason for this choice was the KC-10's ability to operate from shorter runways.

Watch Video: 747 Tanker

Dreamlifter/Large Cargo Freighter (LCF)

In 2003, Boeing decided to use air transport as the primary method of transporting parts for the new 787 widebody airliner as ocean shipping was considered too time-consuming. As a result, over the following years, four second-hand passenger 747-400 aircraft were converted into an outsize configuration in order to fly sub-assemblies from their manufacturing plants in Japan and Italy to the United States, first to Charleston, South Carolina, and then to Everett, Washington for final assembly. Although officially designated the Large Cargo Freighter (LCF), the aircraft was named Dreamlifter, a reference to the 787's name, the Dreamliner, in 2006. It was partially designed by Boeing's Moscow bureau and Boeing Rocketdyne with the swing tail designed in partnership with Gamesa Aeronautica of Spain.

The conversion was carried out by Evergreen Aviation Technologies Corporation in Taiwan, a joint venture between Evergreen Group's EVA Air and General Electric. It was

Due to its ungainly form, and exacerbated by the fact that the need for immediate testing resulted in the first Dreamlifter model remaining unpainted for some time, Boeing's president Scott Carson jokingly apologised to Joe Sutter, designer of the original 747, by saying, "Sorry for what we did to your plane." (Boeing)

Watch Video: Dreamlifter

much more economical for Boeing to purchase used 747s and convert them than to construct these aircraft from scratch. Moreover, modifying existing planes requires less regulation and flight testing by aviation authorities. Had the Dreamlifter been a completely new aircraft entirely designed by Boeing, it would have taken the same years-long development and testing required for a new design like the 787. Approving modifications to an existing aircraft is significantly faster than approving a brand new (and untested) aircraft design.

As part of the flight test programme, the Dreamlifter delivered major sections of the 787 from partner sites around the world to the Boeing American factory in Everett, Washington, for final assembly. After 437 flight-test hours and 639 hours of ground testing since its maiden flight on September 9, 2006, the aircraft was granted type certification on June 2, 2007 from the U.S. FAA. The Dreamlifter's unusual appearance has drawn comparisons to the Oscar Mayer 'Wienermobile' (hot-dog-shaped motor vehicle) and the 'Spruce Goose', the giant Hughes H-4 Hercules flying boat built during World War II.

Of the four Dreamlifters acquired, three became operational in 2008, followed by the fourth aircraft in 2010. On July 1, 2020, a Dreamlifter delivered 500,000 facemasks

The Dreamlifter is similar in concept to the Super Guppy and Airbus A300-600ST Beluga outsize cargo aircraft, which are also used for the transportation of wings and fuselage sections. (Boeing)

The rear section can be folded away to the side to allow loading from the rear. The Dreamlifter does not have a cargo nose door. (Boeing)

The Dreamlifter's interior. In its bulging fuselage, it can hold three times the volume of a 747-400F freighter. (Boeing)

The Dreamlifter uses a DBL-100 cargo loader for loading 787 parts such as the wings into its fuselage. This system was designed and built by the Canadian firm, TLD at its facility at Sherbrooke, Quebec, and is the longest in the world at 118 feet (36 metres). (Boeing)

to Salt Lake City International Airport, Utah, to be used by Utah schoolchildren and teachers as part of the state's response to the Coronavirus pandemic.

YAL-1A Airborne Laser

From 1975 to 1984, the U.S. Department of Defense used a Boeing NKC-135, a Boeing 707 derivative converted into a flying testbed for various systems, for its airborne laser (ABL) lab programme. Designed as an airborne missile defence system to destroy enemy missiles, the modified aircraft carried a 10.6 micrometre carbon dioxide laser. The tests included successful interceptions of small air-to-air missiles (such as the AIM-9 Sidewinder) and of drones (radio-controlled aircraft). Despite its combat potential, the system did not get beyond the experimental stage. However, the threat posed by Soviet-designed SCUD ballistic missiles during the 1991 Gulf War (Operation *Desert Storm*) eventually reignited interest in an airborne laser system, resulting in the development of a new aircraft, designated the Boeing YAL-1A.

As a result, the Department of Defense modified a former Air India 747-400F by equipping it with a megawatt-class chemical oxygen iodine laser (COIL). Initiated by the U.S. Air Force and eventually transferred to the Missile Defense Agency (MDA), the development of the system was a cooperation between various contractors: Boeing Defense, Space & Security provided the aircraft, the management team and the systems integration processes, Northrop Grumman supplied the COIL, and Lockheed Martin designed the nose turret and the fire control system.

Watch Video: Airborne Laser

The YAL-1A's ABL was primarily designed as a missile defence system to destroy enemy ballistic missiles such as the SCUD while these were in boost phase after their launch (which is the portion of the missile's flight during which the booster/engine operates until reaching peak velocity) while the aircraft

Air-to-air refuelling of a YAL-1A (right) by a KC-135 during a test flight. To refuel the laser, the YAL-1A would have to land. The aircraft itself could have been refuelled in flight, which would have enabled it to stay airborne for long periods. Preliminary operational plans called for the ABL to be escorted by fighters and possibly electronic warfare aircraft. The ABL aircraft would likely have had to orbit near potential launch sites (located in hostile countries) for long periods, flying a figure-eight pattern that allowed the aircraft to keep the laser aimed toward the missiles. (Boeing)

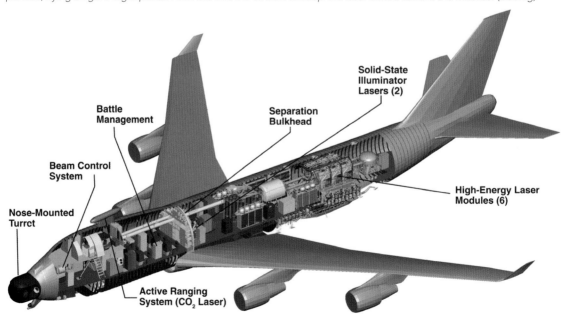

Cutaway rendering of the YAL-1A's interior. (Boeing)

YAL-1A Airborne Laser in flight with the mirror unstowed. (U.S. Missile Defense Agency)

Artist impression of two YAL-1As shooting down ballistic missiles. The laser beams are highlighted red for visibility (in reality, they would be invisible to the naked eye). (U.S. Air Force)

loitered at an altitude of 40,000 feet (12,000 metres). The enemy missile launch was detected by a reconnaissance system such as satellite or AWACS aircraft and threat data was transmitted to the YAL-1A aircraft by data link communications system. In addition, a suite of infrared, wide-field telescopes installed along the length of the aircraft's fuselage detected the missile plume at ranges up to several hundred miles. The ABL's pointing and tracking system tracked the missile and provided launch and predicted impact locations. The turret at the aircraft nose then swivelled toward the target and a 1.5-metre telescope mirror system inside the nose focused the laser beam onto the missile. The laser beam then locked onto the missile, which was destroyed near its launch area within seconds of lock-on.

An optical engineer at the U.S. Air Force Research Laboratory evaluates the interaction of multiple lasers to be used aboard the Airborne Laser (ABL). The laser did not burn through or disintegrate its target, it heated the missile skin, thus weakening it and causing failure from high-speed flight stress. The laser used chemical fuel similar to rocket propellant to generate the high laser power. Each YAL-1A was to carry enough laser fuel for up to 20 shots, or up to 40 low-power shots against fragile tactical ballistic missiles (TBMs). In theory, the laser could also be used against hostile fighter aircraft, cruise missiles or even low-earth-orbit satellites. (U.S. Air Force/Research Laboratory's Directed Energy Directorate)

Close-up of the target illumination laser. It was tested for the first time during a flight on March 15, 2007. Its pointing and tracking system successfully tracked and 'hit' its target, which was a Boeing NC-135E Big Crow test aircraft that had been specially modified with a 'signboard' target on its fuselage. The test proved the system's general ability to track an airborne target and measure and compensate for atmospheric distortion. (Boeing)

After conducting several simulations and tests on the ground, in-flight testing of the YAL-1A's laser including the tracking of missiles began in 2007. In early 2010, it destroyed two different test missiles in flight. However, due to various factors the ABL was not considered viable as then-secretary of defense, Robert M. Gates, summarised in 2011: "I don't know anybody at the Department of Defense … who thinks that this programme should, or would, ever be operationally deployed. The reality is that you would need a laser something like 20 to 30 times more powerful than the chemical laser in the plane right now to be able to get any distance from the launch site to fire … So, right now the ABL would have to orbit inside the borders of Iran in order to be able to try and use its laser to shoot down that missile in the boost phase. And if you were to operationalise this you would be looking at ten to 20 747s, at a billion and a half dollars apiece, and $100 million a year to operate. And there's nobody in uniform that I know who believes that this is a workable concept."

After the ABL's cancellation in December 2011, the YAL-1A aircraft made its final flight three months later and landed at Davis-Monthan Air Force Base in Tucson, Arizona. Here it was mothballed at the 'Boneyard' of the 309th Aerospace Maintenance and Regeneration Group. With no future use in sight, and after the removal of all usable parts, the jet was ultimately scrapped in September of 2014. After the programme's end, the Department of Defense incorporated its findings into a study of mounting missile defence lasers on unmanned aerial vehicles (UAVs) capable of flying above the altitude limits of the converted airliner.

The Jumbo for World Leaders

When attending international conferences, summits, or making visits abroad, world leaders and heads of states regularly use large jets to a rrive in style when representing their people and flying their country's flag. As meaningful symbols of national identity abroad, these aircraft enjoy a prestige resembling that of the world-famous but long-retired British royal yacht *Britannia* when it sailed into foreign ports with Queen Elizabeth II on board. Among these government jets, one always stands out in particular, and that is the Jumbo.

The Flying White House: *Air Force One*

Probably the most recognisable government aircraft in the world is the American president's Boeing 747. Contrary to what is widely thought, there is no jet with the name 'Air Force One'. An aircraft becomes *Air Force One* when the American president boards it and flies on it. Therefore, any aircraft can become *Air Force One*. The current presidential air transport fleet consists of two specially configured Boeing 747-200Bs (tail numbers 28000 and 29000) carrying the air force designation VC-25. When the president is aboard either aircraft, the radio call sign is 'Air Force One'. The two aircraft often operate in conjunction with 'Marine One' helicopters, which ferry him to airports whenever a vehicle motorcade would be inappropriate. On some occasions, the vice-president flies with VC-25As using the call sign 'Air Force Two'. The flights are preceded by an aerial convoy of several cargo transports carrying the helicopters, motorcade vehicles, and other equipment required by the presidential entourage.

After a presidential inauguration resulting in a change in office, the outgoing president is provided transport on a VC-25A aircraft to his home destination. The jets have also been used to transport deceased former presidents, as each has an area where chairs and tables can be removed and the casket laid in their place. A specially designed hydraulic lifter moves the casket up to the port side aft door to enter the aircraft. The tradition of placing the caskets in

Watch Video:
Air Force One

the passenger cabin dates back to the assassination of John F. Kennedy in Dallas in 1963, when his wife Jackie and the crew did not want his body placed in the cargo hold for the flight home to Washington.

VC-25A Air Force One *overflies Mount Rushmore with the sculpted heads of presidents George Washington, Thomas Jefferson, Theodore Roosevelt and Abraham Lincoln. This very special 747 is a prominent symbol of the American presidency. With the White House and presidential seal, it is among the most recognised presidential symbols. The jet has often appeared in popular culture and fiction, including the action movie* Air Force One *starring Harrison Ford. (U.S. Air Force)*

Background and Development

American presidential air transport began in 1944, when Franklin D. Roosevelt travelled aboard a Douglas C-54 Skymaster, designated VC-54 and nicknamed the 'Sacred Cow'. While the radio call sign 'Air Force One' was first used in the 1950s, President John F. Kennedy's VC-137 (a modified Boeing 707) became the first aircraft to be popularly known as *Air Force One*.

By 1985, when the two presidential VC-137 jets had been in service for 23 and 13 years respectively, the U.S. Air Force began searching for an eventual replacement. The new aircraft was to have at least three engines and an unrefuelled minimum range of 6,000 miles (9,700 kilometres). When Boeing with its Jumbo and McDonnell Douglas with the DC-10 competed for the prestigious contract to build the next presidential aircraft, the former became the winner. Construction began during Ronald Reagan's administration (1981-9). The

two VC-25As were completed in 1986 and first flew in 1987. The interior designs were created by First Lady Nancy Reagan, who used designs reminiscent of the American Southwest. Problems with interior wiring for the communications systems delayed delivery of the two jets until 1990, during the administration of Reagan's successor, George H. W. Bush.

The two VC-25As jets are operated and maintained by the Presidential Airlift Group, and are assigned to Air Mobility Command's 89th Airlift Wing located at Joint Base Andrews, Maryland, near Washington, D.C.

Design

The two VC-25A aircraft are extensively modified Boeing 747-200s. Powered by four General Electric CF6-80C2B1 jet engines with 252 kN (56,700 lbf) thrust per engine, both jets incorporate state-of-the-art avionics and communications equipment. The wiring is covered with heavy shielding for protection

Left: *George H. W. Bush was the first American president to use the two VC-25As as Air Force One. After him, the two jets served his successors Bill Clinton, George W. Bush, Barack Obama, Donald Trump and Joe Biden. (U.S. National Archives)*

Right: *Air Force One also boasts a conference room, originally designed as a situation room, but now used for meeting with staff while in flight. This room includes a 50-inch television screen which can be used for teleconferencing. The aircraft has fully equipped office areas with telecommunications systems. (U.S. National Archives)*

from a nuclear electromagnetic pulse (EMP) in the event of a nuclear attack. Both jets have electronic countermeasures (ECMs) to jam enemy radar, flares to avoid heat-seeking missiles, and chaff to avoid radar-guided missiles. For security reasons, many of the VC-25's other capabilities are highly classified. Other differences between the presidential VC-25 and the standard Boeing 747 airliner variant are the self-contained baggage loader, front and aft air-stairs, and the in-flight refuelling capability.

Each VC-25A cost approximately $325 million. According to the U.S. Air Force, the operating cost for each VC-25A in 2014 was $210,877 per hour. The maximum speed is at least 630 mph or 1,010 km/h (Mach 0.92). (U.S. Dept. of Defense)

A U.S. Navy SEAL team helps secure the airfield as President George W. Bush arrives on Air Force One at Al Asad Air Base, Iraq, on September 3, 2007. This jet has always been considered a target for terrorists. (U.S. Dept. of Defense)

Left: *The president's and first lady's private quarters in the front of the aircraft. The couches can fold out into beds. (U.S. National Archives)*
Right: *President Barack Obama plays with his dog in a corridor aboard Air Force One. (White House/Pete Souza)*

The aircraft's front section is informally called the 'White House', a reference to the president's official residence. The president's executive suite includes sleeping quarters with two couches that can be converted into beds, lavatory and shower, vanity closet, double sink, and an office, from where he can address the nation. Originally, the office did not have the equivalent of high-speed internet suitable for broadcasting a video address. This capability was added after the terror attacks on September 11, 2001, during which *Air Force One* had to land at Barksdale Air Force Base, Louisiana, for President George W. Bush to address the nation. A conference and dining room is also available for the president, his family, and staff. With a crew of 30, the VC-25As can accommodate more than 70 passengers. The jets have separate quarters for guests, senior staff, security personnel, and the secret service. The news media is located in the aft area of the main deck. Protocol states that one may wander aft of one's assigned seat, but not forward of it (towards the president's area).

Two galleys can provide up to 100 meals at any one sitting. The president gets a personal menu. The VC-25A has six passenger lavatories, including disabled access facilities, a rest area, a small aircrew galley, and a compartment outfitted with medical equipment and supplies for minor medical emergencies. Every flight is staffed by a doctor and nurse.

The Future

After more than three decades of service, both VC-25A jets, which are based on the 747-200 and which most airlines have retired, are among the oldest, yet best-maintained Jumbos in service. The U.S. Air Force has planned to replace both jets with two new ones based on the latest 747-variant, the 747-8 Intercontinental, designated VC-25B. To reduce the acquisition costs for the new aircraft, the decision was made not to order them from Boeing, but to purchase two existing but brand-new 747-8s. These had originally been built for the Russian airline Transaero, but were never delivered due to that company's bankruptcy. As the air force is not disclosing the value of the deal, it is impossible to know exactly how much money was saved by buying the undelivered 747-8s. The two new jets are currently being converted into presidential aircraft and are expected to enter service by the mid-2020s After the retirement of the two active VC-25As, these could become treasured major exhibits in aviation museums.

9/11: Inside *Air Force One*

September 11, 2001 began as a normal day, when President George W. Bush attended an event at Emma E. Booker Elementary School in Sarasota, Florida, as part of a statewide education tour. He was suddenly interrupted when a passenger jet hit the South Tower

of the World Trade Center in New York City. Bush was then rushed to his presidential jet VC-25A (tail number 29000), which was standing by at the nearby Sarasota-Bradenton International Airport, and took off to fly back to Washington, D.C.

At this point, it became apparent that terrorists had hijacked several commercial airliners travelling in U.S. airspace. This meant that aircraft were now weapons, while civilian and government buildings were targets. In addition, it was feared that the terrorists were also targeting *Air Force One*.

The terrorist attacks on the World Trade Center and the Pentagon on September 11, 2001 shocked the world. (FEMA/Bri Rodriguez)

President George W. Bush has tension and concern written all over his face during the tragic events of 9/11. (U.S. National Archives)

Left: *During the flight back to Washington D.C., there is great uncertainty on board* Air Force One *about whether the aircraft could also become a terrorist target. (U.S. National Archives)*

Right: *Escort by F-16 fighter aircraft during the flight from Offutt Air Force Base, Nebraska, to Andrews Air Force Base, Maryland. (U.S. National Archives)*

Shortly after takeoff, the flight crew received an ominous warning from air traffic control (ATC) that a passenger jet was close and unresponsive to calls. Colonel (ret.) Mark Tillman was *Air Force One*'s senior pilot in charge on that fateful day. During a lecture that he gave at the U.S. Air Force Museum, Dayton, Ohio – Wings & Things Guest Lecture Series – in 2012, he recalled his 9/11 experience: "I started heading across Florida, heading towards Washington, D.C.; at this point now, Jacksonville Center advised us, 'Air Force One, you have traffic above you descending into you. Are you aware of that?' 'No, we're not aware of that at all.'"

In response to this reported potential threat, Tillman steered the presidential jet over the Gulf of Mexico to test whether the suspicious aircraft would follow: "He [the other jet] kept descending toward the Jacksonville area. As it turns out, it was an airliner that had lost his transponder and then had not made the subsequent radio call to the next sector of Jacksonville. He was not a threat."

At the same time, the U.S. Federal Aviation Administration ordered all aircraft that were still in the air to land immediately to find out how many of these had been hijacked. President Bush had wanted to return to

Washington, but after news that an aircraft had crashed into the Pentagon, the decision was made to head to Louisiana and land at Barksdale Air Force Base.

A potential threat scenario (which later proved incorrect) came again when Tillman received a message warning of an imminent attack on *Air Force One*: "At this point, I was a strong believer in the 'big sky theory' that no one was going to find me, but I was not going to take the chance, so I asked for a fighter escort."

President Bush, White House Chief of Staff Andy Card (left) and Admiral Richard Mies conduct a video teleconference at Offutt Air Force Base in Nebraska. (U.S. National Archives)

President Bush delivers remarks on the terrorist attacks from Barksdale Air Force Base in Louisiana, before departing for Offutt Air Force Base in Nebraska. (U.S. National Archives)

A short time later he received the message that two Air National Guard F-16 fighters were joining up: "The best radio call I ever heard in my life was, 'Air Force One, this is Calvary 45, flight of two, we are your cover, ETA [estimated time of arrival] three minutes.' After landing at Barksdale, Bush addressed the nation in a recorded speech about the unfolding national crisis. After a two-hour stay, *Air Force One* left for Offutt Air Force Base, Nebraska, where the president was taken into an underground bunker designed to withstand a nuclear blast. There he held a teleconference call with Vice-President Cheney, National Security Advisor Condoleezza Rice, Defense Secretary Donald Rumsfeld, CIA Director George Tenet, and others. After an hour, Tillman met his commander-in-chief aboard *Air Force One*: "As I got on the plane, the president was already on the plane, standing at the top of the stairs, up by the cockpit, and he just looked at me and said, 'Tillman, it's time to get home.' Absolutely, boom! I jumped in the cockpit [and] started heading across the country." Escorted by fighters, the

presidential jet flew home while practically being the only aircraft in the sky.

"We descended on Washington D.C.; we finally could see what exactly had happened. We could see the Pentagon smoldering. Prior to that, we had seen footage on television, but we hadn't seen anything real at this point." After landing at Andrews Air Force Base in Maryland near the U.S. capital, President Bush thanked the crew for bringing *Air Force One* home safely.

Japanese Government Aircraft

After using chartered aircraft from Japan Airlines (JAL) for official overseas trips, the Japanese government ordered two 747-400s in the late 1980s. Delivered in 1991, they were used to transport the prime minister, the emperor (*Tennō*) and the empress, and other high-ranking officials to state visits, summits and international conferences. The jets were officially designated as 'exclusive Japanese government aircraft' (*Nippon-koku seifu sen'yōki*) carrying the radio call signs 'Japanese Air Force One' and

After its safe return flight from Florida, Air Force One touches down at Andrews Air Force Base in Maryland. The world had changed in just a few hours. (U.S. National Archives)

President Bush disembarks from Air Force One at Andrews AFB on the afternoon of September 11, 2001 and is met by U.S. Air Force personnel on the ramp. (U.S. National Archives)

'Japanese Air Force Two' when in official use, and 'Cygnus One' and 'Cygnus Two' when used unofficially, such as on training flights.

The aircraft had state-of-the-art communications technology, although the nature and extent of this is unknown; further details have also never been released. They were also to be used for emergency airlift of Japanese nationals staying overseas, international emergency relief aid operations, and contributions to United Nations peacekeeping operations.

The aircraft had an office area for the prime minister in the front part on the main deck, which could be modified for the imperial family or other VIPs. The cabin behind the office had lie-flat seating for senior officials in a 2–3–2 configuration, a separate enclosed VIP cabin including two seats, a conference table with seats that folded down into beds, and a secretarial area with office equipment. The main cabin was normally used as a seating area for the media, with seating equivalent to airline short-haul business class seating (also 2–3–2 configuration), and a table at the front to be used for in-flight press conferences. These cabins could be used as passenger seating on evacuation missions. The upper deck had seating equivalent to airline economy class seating (3–3 and 2–3 configuration), which was used for communications and crew rest. Painted with red and gold stripes along the fuselage and red sun insignia on the tail and wings, both jets were actually commanded by the Special Airlift Group of the Japanese Air Self-Defense Force (SDF) at Chitose Air Base.

Both aircraft could only be used for government business, and not for personal travel by the imperial family or the prime minister. The aircrafts' missions included flying into a hostage situation in Algeria in 2013, and travelling to Bangladesh following a terrorist attack in 2016. In both cases they brought back the bodies of Japanese citizens who had been killed.

In 2019, the Japanese government replaced its 747-400s with a pair of Boeing 777-300ERs. During their time in service, the

Both Japanese Air Force One jets in formation flight (military markings No. 20-1101 and No. 20-1102). They usually flew together on government missions, with one serving as the primary transport and the other as a backup with maintenance personnel on board. They were powered by General Electric CF6-80C2B1F engines. (Japanese Ministry of Defense/Self Defense Force)

Soldiers of the 1st Battalion, 3rd Infantry Regiment fire cannons in salute as Japanese Prime Minister Shinzo Abe arrives in a motorcade to leave Joint Base Andrews after his state visit to the U.S. on April 30, 2015.
(U.S. Air Force / Kevin Wallace)

One of the two Japanese Air Force Ones *during a night landing at Chitose Air Force Base in northern Japan. (Kosuke Ota)*

747s completed 349 flights and visited 269 locations in 100 countries. The fate of the two jets is uncertain.

Chinese *Air Force One*

For many years, the government of the People's Republic of China has been using Boeing 747-400s from Air China for international travel. At least one of them has been specially retrofitted for official flights by upgrading its First and Business classes with the addition of prefabricated modules. After returning home the interior is restored to the original airliner configuration. In late 2014, a new 747-8 Intercontinental (registration No. B-2479) left the Boeing factory in Everett and underwent thorough cabin modifications to VIP standard in Hamburg, Germany. In October 2016, the aircraft became the official *Air Force One* of President Xi Jinping

and the Chinese government for state visits abroad. Operated by Air China, the jet features a luxurious master suite including an executive office for the president and the first lady, a main lounge for ministers and

The President of the People's Republic of China, Xi Jinping, arrives with his wife, First Lady Peng Liyua, on a state visit to Ecuador on November 17, 2016, where they are received with honours. (Cancillería del Ecuador)

top aides, a medical centre, and a secret service command room. Moreover, the 747-8 has all the security and communication features to ensure real-time command and conferencing, and defence against threats from air or ground.

Turkish Government Aircraft

In 2018, the Emir of Qatar, Sheikh Tamim bin Hamad Al Thani, gave a Boeing 747-8, worth an estimated $400 million to Turkish President Recep Tayyip Erdogan. This gift was a symbol of "Thani's special love for Erdogan", according to Turkey's state-run broadcaster TRT. It is not known how the Turkish president expressed his gratitude or what he did in return. The jet had previously served in Qatar's VIP Amiri Flight fleet, which caters exclusively to Qatar's royal family and other high-ranking government staff. Outfitted to carry only 76 passengers and a crew of 18, this very luxurious 747-8 features staterooms, lounges, boardrooms, First Class seating, state-of-the-art security and even a medical centre.

President Xi Jinping gives a short speech upon arrival. His wife Peng Liyua stands to his right. (Cancillería del Ecuador)

With the 747-8, Turkey owns not only one of the largest, but also one of the most modern government aircraft in the world. (Hajime Suzuki)

Saddam Hussein's luxuriously outfitted 747SP. During a stopover in London in 1986, his pilot Captain Al-Wahabi decided to leave the jet and flee, as he no longer wanted to be exposed to the aggression and unpredictability of the Iraqi dictator. This successful escape was kept a secret, until Al-Wahabi turned public with his story after Hussein was removed from power in 2003. On the eve of the Second Gulf War (Operation Desert Storm), the dictator had this Jumbo (YI-ALM) and an Iraqi Airways 747-200M (YI-AGP) flown to Tozeur-Nefta International Airport, Tunisia, in January 1991 to save them from bombardment. Hussein never had the jets flown back to Iraq. He was hanged in 2006, and to this day, both Jumbos are still stored in Tunisia. (Petr Popelář)

Queen Elizabeth II and Prince Philip disembark from a British Airways Concorde at Bergstrom Air Force Base near Austin, Texas, on their state visit to the United States in 1991. Occasionally, the supersonic Concorde was used to transport the royal family and the prime minister, particularly to international conferences abroad. In 2012, Prime Minister David Cameron used a Boeing 747-400 operated by charter airline Atlas Air to visit countries in South East Asia. (U.S. Air Force/SRA Jerry Wilson)

Other Government Jumbos

In addition to the United States, Japan, and China, a number of other governments also use or have used the 747 as a government aircraft or for VIP transport, including Argentina, Bahrain, Brunei, India, Iran, Iraq, Kuwait, Oman, Pakistan, Qatar, Saudi Arabia, South Korea, the United Arab Emirates, and the United Kingdom. Some of these jets received a custom-made VIP interior with a luxurious interior. Examples of such models include the 747s of Bahrain or the Saudi Prince al-Walid ibn Talal Al Saud. In addition, several Boeing 747-8s have been ordered by Boeing Business Jet for conversion to VIP transports for several unidentified customers.

Ernest Angley Ministries Boeing 747SP

In 2004, Ernest Angley Ministries purchased a Boeing 747SP, which had previously been owned by Trans World Airlines, American

Boeing can customise the interior of the 747 (and other models) at the customer's request. This includes high-quality fittings with a high level of comfort and luxury. (Boeing)

Sleeping quarters aboard the Star Triple Seven. (John Padgett)

Airlines, and the United Arab Emirates government (Royal Flight). Named *Star Triple Seven* (P4-FSH), it was used to transport missionaries and humanitarian aid internationally. After withdrawal from service due to technical problems in 2018, the aircraft was placed in storage at Pinal Airpark, Arizona.

Iron Maiden's *Ed Force One*

For their 'Somewhere Back in Time World Tour' in 2008 and 2009, the English heavy metal band Iron Maiden commissioned an Astraeus Airlines Boeing 757 as transport. The jet was repainted in a special Iron Maiden livery and converted into a combi

The Boeing 747SP Star Triple Seven in storage. (John Padgett)

configuration enabling it to carry the band, the crew, and stage production. This allowed the group to perform in countries previously deemed logistically unreachable. Named *Ed Force One* after a competition on the band's website, the aircraft was flown by band member Bruce Dickinson, who was also a commercial airline pilot for Astraeus. A different 757 with altered livery was used for the 2011 'The Final Frontier World Tour'. For the 2016 'The Book of Souls World Tour', Iron Maiden chose a former Air France 747-400, which meant that Dickinson had to undertake type conversion to fly the larger jet. Supplied by Air Atlanta Icelandic (TF-AAK), the Jumbo was customised by Volga-Dnepr Gulf, which allowed for more space without the necessity of undergoing a significant conversion to carry the band's equipment.

Cosmic Girl

Cosmic Girl is a Boeing 747-400 airliner, which was delivered to Virgin Atlantic (Virgin Group) in 2001. The jet was transferred to Virgin Galactic in 2015 to be used as a launch platform ('mothership') for *LauncherOne*, an air-launched rocket, designed to carry smallsat payloads (miniaturised satellites) of up to 300 kilograms (660 pounds) into orbit.

Air-launch of satellite-carrying rockets from an airborne aircraft is considered a more cost-effective alternative compared to satellite

Iron Maiden's Ed Force One, a Boeing 747-400, wearing the band's livery as used during 'The Book of Souls World Tour' in 2016. The jet was named after Iron Maiden's mascot, Eddie the Head, who is depicted on the rudder. (Chung Kwok)

launches with a much larger and more expensive rocket from a launch pad on the ground.

The *LauncherOne* attachment pylon is situated on the left wing, where on a normal 747 the fifth engine attachment point is located for ferrying engines. This point is located between the fuselage and the left inboard engine. *LauncherOne* would be dropped from *Cosmic Girl* at a height of 35,000 feet (11,000 metres). The maximum payload limit for *LauncherOne* operations on the aircraft is 400 kilograms (880 pounds).

In 2017, the jet was transferred to the orbital launch subsidiary, Virgin Orbit, and its livery updated to Virgin Orbit livery. On its first flight, on May 25, 2020, *LauncherOne* failed to reach space after its release from *Cosmic Girl*, over the Pacific Ocean. The second launch on January 17, 2021, successfully delivered ten miniaturised satellites (cubesats) to low Earth orbit (LEO).

Stratolaunch *Roc*

The *Roc* is a twin-fuselage aircraft, which was built for the private American company Stratolaunch Systems by Scaled Composites (owned by Northrop Grumman). It was

Cosmic Girl carrying the LauncherOne rocket out to the Pacific Ocean from California for the second launch on January 17, 2021. (Glenn Beltz, CC BY 2.0)

designed to air-launch rockets such as the Pegasus (Northrop Grumman) or a Stratolaunch-proposed Medium Launch Vehicle into orbit. Rockets like these can carry payloads (including satellites) with a weight of up to 225 tonnes into orbit, thus making *Roc* a more capable (yet more complex and expensive) launch platform than *Cosmic Girl*.

The twin-fuselage Stratolaunch design features the longest wingspan ever flown, at 385 feet (117 meters), even surpassing the World War II-era Hughes H-4 Hercules flying boat of 321 feet (98 meters). The massive aircraft is powered by six Pratt & Whitney PW4056 engines positioned on pylons outboard of each fuselage, providing 252.4 kN (56,750 lbf) of thrust per engine. (Stratolaunch)

Announced in 2011 and rolled out in May 2017, the aircraft has a twin-fuselage configuration, each 238 feet (73 metres) long and supported by 12 main landing gear wheels and two nose gear wheels, for a total of 28 wheels.

Watch Video: Stratolaunch Roc

Besides performing high-speed flight test services, Roc *could carry rockets to deliver satellites into orbit, or launch a reusable spaceplane such as Black Ice, capable of transporting astronauts or cargo to and from low Earth orbit and to and from the International Space Station (ISS). (Stratolaunch)*

The flight crew is accommodated in the right fuselage cockpit. The left unmanned fuselage cockpit is used as storage space for mission-specific support equipment.

Roc has the longest wingspan ever flown, at 385 feet (117 metres). With a maximum takeoff weight of 1,300,000 pounds (590 tonnes), it is intended to carry a 500,000-pound (225-tonne) payload (rocket) and release it at 35,000 feet (11,000 metres).

The aircraft has flown twice, the last time on April 29, 2021. Following the death of Stratolaunch founder Paul Allen in October 2018, the company announced it would halt the development of its air-launched vehicles. After ceasing operations in May 2019, Stratolaunch placed all company assets, including the aircraft, for sale. Cerberus Capital Management acquired Stratolaunch Systems, including the aircraft, in October 2019. Shortly thereafter, it was announced that the new focus of Stratolaunch LLC would be on offering high-speed flight test services.

Within Scaled Composites, the Stratolaunch's model number is M351. It is named "Roc" after Sinbad's Roc, the mythical bird so big it could carry an elephant. (Stratolaunch)

In order to reduce the development costs, many of the aircraft systems have been adopted from the Boeing 747-400, including the engines, avionics, flight deck, landing gear, and other systems. (Stratolaunch)

In Search of the Pan Am
Clipper Juan T. Trippe

The second Jumbo ever built was N747PA, which first flew on April 11, 1969, just two months after the first one, the *City of Everett*.

After being used as a test aircraft by Boeing, she was delivered to Pan Am on October 3, 1970, several months after the airline had received its first 747. Originally christened *Clipper America*, she was renamed *Clipper Sea Lark*, and finally *Clipper Juan T. Trippe*, thus

The former Clipper Juan T. Trippe was converted into a restaurant in Namyangju, South Korea. The colour scheme resembles that of the American Air Force One jet. This photo was taken long after the restaurant had been closed and shows an advanced stage of decay. (Yunjin Lee)

The dining area of the 'Jumbo Restaurant' showing the partially modified interior. (Yunjin Lee)

Although the Clipper Juan T. Trippe *lost much of her substance, she defied all reports and rumours that she was scrapped and is now awaiting a future as a church and museum. There is an elevator attached just outside the 2L door. (Yunjin Lee)*

honouring Pan Am's founder. The jet's iconic tail number, N747PA, was one of the most recognised tail numbers among the airline's employees. After Pan Am ceased operations in late 1991, N747PA would keep that registration and fly for two other airlines until 1995.

After the end of her service, she arrived in San Bernardino, California, and was scrapped – but only partially. Most of her large fuselage and parts of her wings were shipped to Namyangju, a suburb of Seoul, South Korea. There, N747PA was reassembled and opened as a restaurant. However, after a few years, the business closed, and in 2010 there were media reports that the days of the *Clipper Juan T. Trippe* were finally numbered – she was ultimately going to be scrapped.

However, her story does not end here as she managed to escape the cutting torch for a second time: with only parts of her scrapped in 2010, three major fuselage sections were saved,

transported to a different location in the same town, and reassembled, thus making her slightly shorter than a 747SP. Repainted in Korean Air colours, the former *Clipper Juan T. Trippe* has been given a new lease on life as a Christian church and aviation museum – this is certainly welcome news for enthusiasts of Pan Am.

In 2017, a former Pakistan International Airlines 747-300 was converted into a restaurant by Pakistan's Airports Security Force. It is located at Jinnah International Airport, Karachi. A former British Airways 747-200B is parked at the Dunsfold Aerodrome in Surrey, England, and has been used as a movie set for productions such as the 2006 James Bond film, *Casino Royale*. The jet also appears occasionally in the television series *Top Gear*. In 2009, the 'Jumbo Hostel' opened at Arlanda Airport near Stockholm, Sweden. This consists of a former Boeing 747-200 that was converted into a hostel with more than 80 beds.

ON BOARD
THE JUMBO

The Jumbo is not only a means of transportation for global passenger and cargo traffic, but also a highly popular workplace for pilots, flight attendants and the technical staff on the ground. They all proudly contribute to the fine reputation of the famous aircraft.

(johnnypowell.net)

CHAPTER 5

Jan Netzeband's (born 1980) wonderful childhood memories include the adventures he experienced with his father (also a pilot) on his flights around the world. Inspired by this, he began his pilot career at Eurowings in 2004, transferred to Lufthansa Cargo three years later, and has been flying the Boeing 747 for Lufthansa since 2014. (Jan Netzeband)

View from the Cockpit Crew

Senior First Officer Jan Netzeband of Lufthansa describes a Boeing 747 flight from the cockpit crew's perspective: "A typical workday for long-haul pilots begins with the arrival at the base. On our way to the airport, we're already observing the weather and mentally preparing for any adverse conditions such as thunderstorms or fog, high winds or gusting snow, and the associated operational consequences during the flight. Our duty begins with the briefing, which takes place 100 minutes before the scheduled departure time on every long-haul flight. The cockpit and cabin crew are initially briefed separately until the captain brings the two groups together and gets everyone ready for the flight ahead.

"Our briefing includes a review of the flight documents to assess weather conditions at takeoff, during flight, and at landing. Then we make decisions regarding routing, alternate airfields, and fuel requirements. In addition, we assess the technical condition of the aircraft as well as the restrictions of the important airports on the route. We have half an hour for the joint briefing, team-building, introductions, and getting to know each other. After that, we all proceed to the aircraft an hour before departure.

"While our colleagues prepare the aircraft cabin for the passengers, the ground crew performs the refuelling with the ordered amount of kerosene and loads the 747 with cargo, baggage, and food. At the same time, we check the cockpit and make an external visual inspection of the jet to determine its airworthiness. Then we programme the on-board computers with the routing, enter all the relevant data on loading and weight, and calculate the engine power required for takeoff. Finally, we discuss the departure route and our options in the event of system or engine failures during the first phase of the flight. The captain and his deputies ultimately coordinate all ground operations.

"After boarding our passengers and loading cargo, the actual pilot's work begins. Within the two-person cockpit crew, we designate one crew member who is responsible for conducting the flight and steering the aircraft (the Pilot Flying). He is assisted by the second

Extendable slats and landing flaps are used for safe slow flight during takeoff and landing. The picture shows a Lufthansa 747-8 Intercontinental. (Gabor Hajdufi)

pilot, who supervises him and takes care of organisational matters and communication with the air traffic controllers (the Pilot Monitoring). On very long flights, a third pilot joins the two-person cockpit crew. This pilot can take over both positions in flight to give each of the other two crew members a break.

"In accordance with dedicated checklists and precisely defined procedures, we prepare the aircraft for the next phase of the flight. Takeoff, final approach and landing are still particularly demanding due to constantly changing conditions. This is where we have the aircraft in our hands, and this is also where the good-naturedness and agility of our Boeing 747 come into play. Although modern aircraft can also be landed automatically, the general conditions for this pre-programmed algorithm must be optimally suited. Ultimately, the so-called autoland – we also use the autopilot in cruising flight – only comes into play in low wind, heavy fog situations. Such a situation prevails only on very few approaches.

"For us pilots it is important to keep our head 'in front' of the aircraft at all times: we must be focused on goal-oriented prioritisation of tasks and actively seek possible options for adaptive flight execution until the aircraft is parked after landing to avoid surprise disruptions. During the flight, we coordinate and optimise routing, obtain landing permits, document and verify fuel consumption, and adjust altitude and speed to ensure a safe, comfortable, and economical flight.

"In keeping with the motto 'Everything that goes up must come down,' the planning and implementation of approach and landing are always challenging. Even after a long day's work in the cockpit and despite being possibly tired, these two maneuvers once again require our full concentration. Throughout the flight, we closely monitor the conditions for landing at the destination and adjust our options accordingly. Thus, for example, a landing in Boston in a blizzard or in Frankfurt in beautiful weather never happens without an alternative in mind.

"After landing and docking at the gate, the passengers disembark. Then we park our

Top: *A modern Swissair flight simulator that can be moved into various horizontal positions in order to simulate various flight manoeuvres during pilot training. (Swissair/ETH-Bibliothek Zürich/LBS_SR04-032235/CC BY-SA 4.0)*

Middle: *The flight simulator consists of a functioning cockpit dummy and a computer-simulated view out of the window. This advanced technology has nothing in common with the, from today's perspective, primitive simulator that the test pilots of the 747 prototype had to settle for in the 1960s. (Swissair/ETH-Bibliothek Zürich/LBS_SR04-032236/CC BY-SA 4.0)*

Bottom: *A rather tiny but powerful tug pulls the mighty 747 from its place at the gate to the runway. Then the pilots wait for takeoff clearance. (Corendon Hotels & Resorts)*

The two-pilot cockpit of a Lufthansa 747-400. One is the 'Pilot Flying' who controls the aircraft. The other pilot ('Pilot Monitoring') monitors him and takes care of organisational matters and communication with the air traffic controllers. (Lufthansa)

Jumbo in a way that the next crew can take over the aircraft in its usual configuration. Finally, after customs and immigration procedures, we ride together by bus to a local hotel for the night. Depending on the duration of the flight and the subsequent stay at the destination, we can enjoy some time together there. However, the priority is to get enough sleep to be able to begin the upcoming return flight rested and concentrated.

"So much for the blueprint – in real life, nothing rarely goes according to plan, as many unpredictable things can happen. For example, drunk or aggressive passengers have to be identified and, if necessary, prevented from boarding the flight. There may be delays in ground operations due to takeoff time windows or airfield closures. Mini-dramas take place on board, which we have to deal with. If we have to make an unscheduled stopover somewhere – with moderate enthusiasm from the guests – we might have to deal with unexpected weather deterioration at the destination airport. Every flight is different. Ultimately, however, it is precisely the 'salt in the soup' that makes our job so exciting and multifaceted.

A Jumbo on its final approach. When nearly fully loaded, a 747-400 requires a landing distance of about 2,100 metres. (Bo Luan)

"Besides the size of the 747, I am always fascinated by its elegance. Even though through years of experience you develop a very good feeling for the power, mass, and dimensions of your aircraft, the actual size is experienced primarily on the ground and when you walk through the cabin.

The 747 combines the reliability and good-naturedness of an old tractor with the maneuverability and nimbleness of a Porsche 911. For us pilots, it is simply beautiful and is excellent to fly. For our guests, it is still one of the safest aircraft in the sky.

The 747 is simply a flying legend. Anyone who studies its history will be amazed again and again. Even after all its evolutionary stages since 1969, it has remained true to its original character. She almost harks back to the 'old days', an era full of great pioneering achievements."

Jan Netzeband's colleague Maximilian Reuter recalls a special experience as a 747 pilot: "One of the most impressive experiences with the Boeing 747 is related to the evacuation flights of the German Foreign Office during the Coronavirus crisis in mid-April 2020. We flew one of the last rescue flights of German holidaymakers from Christchurch, New Zealand, with a stopover in Bangkok, Thailand. The New Zealand embassy asked us to fly a circle over the city as a farewell. From the cockpit, hundreds of glowing cell phone displays could be seen in the falling dusk as we said goodbye, a very poignant moment. The 11-hour flight with its route over Sydney and then across Australia was also a real experience.

"When you're sitting in a 747, there's never the slightest doubt that you'll eventually arrive safely at your destination. It always gives you – even in the remotest corners of the earth – the security of having a very reliable partner at your side.

"A friend of my parents was in China in October 1980 as captain of a Lufthansa Boeing 747. On the return flight, a panda bear was to be transported for the Frankfurt Zoo and the crew was given small stuffed panda bears as souvenirs. On October 16, 1980 I first

Maximilian Reuter began gliding at the age of 14. Inspired by club colleagues, he started his training as a commercial pilot at the Lufthansa Fliegerschule in Bremen in 2002, which he completed in 2004. After flying on the Boeing 757, the 737 and the Airbus A320, he has been flying the Jumbo since 2014. (Maximilian Reuter)

747 co-pilot (First Officer) Ute Roth-Bünting from Swissair in the early 1990s. While women were part of the cabin crew in the early years, over time they also 'conquered' the cockpit and thus asserted themselves alongside their male colleagues.
(Swissair/ETH-Bibliothek Zürich/LBS_SR04-026453/CC BY-SA 4.0)

saw the light of day and was given this stuffed panda as a cuddly toy a few days later. So, in a sense, the 747 has been serving me faithfully since I was born."

View from the Cabin Crew

By Birgit Horrion (Purser Boeing 747/Airbus 340)

"Even as a child, I had a very emotional relationship with airplanes and always got wanderlust when I saw one in the sky. Of course, the big planes were something very special, because they flew to exotic and faraway destinations. Back then, people just didn't travel by plane, and certainly not with the whole family. My father was a 'HON Circle Member' with Lufthansa's frequent flyer programme; and I loved the little souvenirs from his trips off the plane – 'amenity kits' from the First and Business classes, and candy with the airline's crane logo. Like many others, I dreamed of becoming a stewardess and seeing the world.

"This wish came true when I completed my basic training course with Lufthansa. After initially working on short-haul flights aboard the Airbus 310/300, I discovered the big, wide world on the DC-10. At the end of 1990, after retraining, I transferred to the Jumbo. The focus of the training was on emergency procedures, such as evacuation and firefighting. These procedures are highly individualised on this aircraft due to its additional upper deck. At the

Lufthansa flight attendant Birgit Horrion next to a model of the 747-8 Intercontinental. (Lufthansa)

Safety briefing for the passengers by a flight attendant before takeoff. (Swissair/ETH-Bibliothek Zürich/LBS_SR04-035612/CC BY-SA 4.0)

time, Lufthansa operated the 747-200 and the 747-400. The former still had a spiral staircase to the upper deck, and because of the special location of the emergency exit there, the door to the cockpit had to remain open during takeoff and landing. This procedure was considered a security risk after the terrorist attacks of September 11, 2001, and therefore accelerated the retirement of the 747-200. There were also new things for me to learn in the service area, because the impressive size of the 747's exterior was of course also evident in its interior.

"The preparation for the flight starts at home: the uniform has to be clean and wrinkle-free, the suitcase packed according to the duration of the rotation, and the CMD [cabin mobile device] charged. We use the CMD to prepare for our mission: in an app, we can review all the data and specifics relevant to the flight. In addition, it is useful to take another look at the required emergency procedures.

"I don't get to know my flight colleagues until the briefing on the day of the actual departure. Together we discuss the flight procedure and have the opportunity to ask questions. There is also a review of the cabin crew's knowledge of emergency procedures. After passport and security checks, we board the aircraft and prepare it for the boarding of our passengers. After takeoff we serve a large meal and before landing a second smaller one. On particularly long flights, we also serve a snack. During service breaks, some crew members

A flight attendant serves drinks on board a Jumbo, 1990. Passenger safety and satisfaction are the top priorities for the cabin and cockpit crew. (Swissair/ETH-Bibliothek Zürich/LBS_SR04-002493/CC BY-SA 4.0)

A flight attendant serves a delicious meal in First Class of a Swissair Boeing 747-200 in 1972. The service on board the Jumbo has always set high standards. (Swissair/ETH-Bibliothek Zürich/LBS_SR04-001805/CC BY-SA 4.0)

Happy and relaxed passengers on board a Jumbo jet at a time when smoking was still allowed on aircraft. (Swissair/ETH-Bibliothek Zürich/LBS_SR04-002246/CC BY-SA 4.0)

Warming up meals delivered on board before the flight in one of the galleys during the 1980s. (Swissair/ETH-Bibliothek Zürich/LBS_SR04-001473/CC BY-SA 4.0)

While passengers enjoy the comfort on board, flight attendants take turns resting on long flights in a specially designated crew rest area in the rear section of the jet. (Glenn White)

have an opportunity to take a break. In the tail section of the 747, there is a separate crew area, where we can retire to our bunks to rest. After the second meal, we begin preparing for landing. Depending on the destination, this can be very time-consuming, as we often have to count the alcoholic beverages and enter them in customs lists. All customs containers then have to be sealed, and for some countries lists have to be filled out by the crew. After landing, we say goodbye to our passengers and leave the jet together after completing our work on board.

"In our profession and on every flight, we accompany a wide variety of people on their journey. Sometimes they share their funny, touching or even sad stories with us. During the flight, the 747 is a piece of home not only for us as crew. Often, our guests abroad greet us with the words, 'Home at last!'

"On one very special flight, I had a truly touching experience. On the occasion of the Tokyo Fashion Week a few years ago, we wore 1960s uniforms (yellow and blue dresses with cape and hat) in the cabin. An elderly female passenger approached us and asked for a photo with a flight attendant. She then told us that she had moved from Japan to Germany with her parents when she was a child: during the long flight she was quite frightened, having never flown before. A flight attendant in a cheerful yellow dress took her by the

Birgit Horrion: "And when calm returns after service on a night flight, the passengers are well fed and asleep, the moon shines over the sea outside and the Jumbo brings us safely closer to our destination while gently humming; this is always a very special feeling." (David van Woerkom)

hand and let her 'help' in the service. After this activity, she sat with the crew in the galley. The time on board literally flew by. Her mother finally took a picture of her and the flight attendant who had so touchingly taken care of her. The elderly lady finally told us that she still had this picture today and was now happy to have a second one with a flight attendant in the same yellow dress.

"Like many other flight attendants, I am emotionally attached to 'our Jumbo'. With its pretty nose and elegant curve on its back, it is simply a beautiful aircraft. Its flight characteristics are very smooth, and turbulence is hardly noticeable – this makes working in the cabin very pleasant. And when calm returns after service on a night flight, the passengers are well fed and asleep, the moon shines over the sea outside and the Jumbo brings us safely closer to our destination while gently humming, this is always a very special feeling.

"Our crew in the cabin is characterised above all by trusting teamwork. Because there are set work routines and different working positions in the aircraft, we ensure that all routine work is carried out diligently. In addition, we are very flexible, because everyone takes on any tasks that arise in service and passenger care."

Lufthansa flight attendants in 1960s uniforms described by Birgit Horrion on the occasion of the Tokyo Fashion Week. (Lufthansa)

View from the Technician

John Powell has been an aircraft technician in the industry for more than 40 years with the last 20 on the 747 before retiring in 2020. He remembers his daily work routine at Virgin Atlantic: "As a technician I worked mostly in teams of two technicians and one certifying engineer with additional avionics and a cabin/IFE (in-flight entertainment) team. My working day began at 5 o'clock in the morning. It wasn't unusual to be driving from the hangar to the ramp and see the first arrival taxiing in already, probably the same 747 we had launched the day before.

"The jet had been flying nonstop barring two or three hours on the ground and we were about to go through that cycle again – it always amazed me how much time the 747 spent in the air. Daily and transit inspections were the norm in addition to any other tasks called up by planning. Normally one of us would greet the crew on the headset to get a heads-up on inbound defects and give clearance for brake release (for brake cooling) once the chocks were in, then complete a full walkaround inspection of the airframe while the other two guys oiled and inspected the engines.

John Powell is a keen photographer whose highlight was a picture on the cover of Flight International *magazine – of course it was a Jumbo (page 121). He retired two years early due to COVID. [www.johnnypowell.net]*

Replacement of a worn or defective wheel. The Jumbo has a total of 18 individual wheels. (Swissair/ETH-Bibliothek Zurich/LBS_SR04-002246/CC BY-SA 4.0)

"Once the passengers had left the jet, third parties would service the potable water and toilet system, replace the catering, and clean the cabin. If it was a quick turnaround (two to three hours) the fuel truck would also begin fuelling. Once the freight came off, we inspected the cargo holds for condition and serviceability.

"It wasn't the best place to be on the aircraft with its delicate framework, being tricky to walk on and quite vulnerable to the efforts of an over eager loader: replacing rubber drive belts was a very popular pastime along with roller trays, pallet stops. and cargo liners.

"Back on the ground, the 18 tyres needed the pressures checked, which was not so bad if the aircraft had TPIS (tyre pressure indicating system); otherwise, it meant the use of an old-fashioned hand gauge. At this point any worn tyres or brakes that needed replacing would be called for.

"We then entered the cabin to experience the delights of checking 13 toilets for a good flush, any water leaks and, if we were unlucky, a few blockages to deal with. Other cabin routine included checking and repairing seats, emergency escape floor lighting, emergency equipment, portable oxygen, galley water waste and ovens and fridges. The cabin log would be checked for defects entered by the crew. On quick turnarounds the cabin was a very busy place with usually two catering teams and more than 20 cleaners armed with hoovers and mops, aggravated

Cleaning the huge interior between flights. Preparing for a flight also includes refuelling and loading luggage, cargo and meals for the passengers. These complex activities require well-organised teamwork. (Swissair / ETH-Bibliothek Zürich / LBS_SR04-027965 / CC BY-SA 4.0)

by us doing our job and getting in the way. It made for a lot of banter!

"In the cockpit, we conducted system checks and fluid quantities such as the four hydraulic systems and the auxiliary power unit [APU] oil. The aircraft technical log was checked for additional tasks to be carried out prior to the next flight. If a wheel required changing it could be done in half an hour by two people and a brake unit in approximately one hour.

"Opening up an engine [General Electric CF-6] for maintenance involved two people physically lifting the fan cowls, then using a hand pump to lift the reverser halves. During winter it was a warm place to work next to an engine that had been running for eight hours and the cowls kept the rain off – mostly.

"If you had fuel, freight, and passengers being loaded the height of the engine could drop considerably whilst you were working as the undercarriage legs compressed and the wings drooped. You could get caught out by the engine gradually nestling onto the steps you were standing on. The outbound flight crew would arrive 90 minutes before takeoff and begin their preflight checks. We were on call should they have any problems; sometimes it was like having 15 wives in your kitchen all at once! Nipping back onboard with the passengers already seated to fix a seat or IFE equipment was a challenge, working around the customers trying your best to look professional

whilst some passengers were clearly worried to see an engineer arrive. Lastly, with the technical log completed, all that was left was a signature of acceptance from the captain.

"Working on smaller jets could be a lonely existence, while the Jumbo brought together more manpower working in teams. It was sometimes hard work trying to accomplish goals with the downtime available but very rewarding on a good day as it helped in building friendships and trust between colleagues. The icing on the cake being able to watch the beast roaring down the runway for another on-time departure.

A jacked-up 747 to test the functionality of the landing gear when stationary. (John Powell)

View into the complex interior of an engine after opening the covers. After landing, these stay warm for a long time – very practical for working on them in winter. (Bas Tolsma)

Left: *Removal of the old paint on a 747. (Corendon Hotels & Resorts)*
Right: *The 747 gets a new paint job. This will require around 340 litres of paint. (Corendon Hotels & Resorts)*

"The Jumbo seemed such a natural evolution from the 707 – especially with the later models and proven reliability over years of service. She looked right, on the ground and in the air. From a photographic point of view, it's just got real presence. A little on the dirty side (aerodynamically) dragging water vapour trails and creating enormous pressure buildup which is sometimes seen as a cloud on top of the wings during takeoff and landing."

Photographing the 747-400: From Theory to Practice

By Bas Tolsma

"To prepare the content for teaching a course on aircraft maintenance at a university of applied sciences, I completed an internship at Amsterdam Schiphol Airport beforehand. This gave me an incomparable insight into the work of maintaining the Boeing 747-400,

John Powell enjoyed a 747 takeoff every time it rolled out of the hangar ready to fly. (John Powell)

and this is how I came to appreciate and photograph the Jumbo."

"I was allowed to join a team of mechanics and technicians that would maintain the 747-400 in the hangar. To work with these experienced men and women was marvellous. Tasks would vary from gear changes to electrical troubleshooting to fixing seats and doing high-power engine test runs after repairing and replacing components. Everything I had learned from the theory books started to make sense.

"The aircraft also made me realise that the books we used to teach the students needed updating, we needed better photos and the addition of videos. I brought a GoPro to enrich the theory in the curriculum, filming maintenance tasks, explaining about certain systems, and showing all types of functional checks. It was during this period that I bought a digital camera to document all sorts of technical aspects, from a variety of aircraft, to be used in the classroom. I ended up doing most of that with the GoPro action photo camera and developed a new hobby: photographing the Boeing 747-400 from a maintenance viewpoint.

Knowing the 747s were being withdrawn from use all over the world, it became the focus of my attention for the more unique shots [some of which are adopted in this book]. They now serve as wallpaper in the hangar at school, showing students commercial aircraft maintenance.

"Photographing the 747 offers some challenges; two aspects that stood out for me were its sheer size and working with

Bas Tolsma is a teacher at a Dutch vocational aircraft maintenance course and an aviation photography enthusiast. His profession has enabled him some unique insights in maintaining the Boeing 747. (Bas Tolsma)

Top: *A 747-400 during night maintenance. The technicians and mechanics work in shifts to make the aircraft operational on time for all flight schedules. (Bas Tolsma)*

Middle: *Close-up of the two front cockpit windows. These have to withstand the high flight speeds, enormous temperature fluctuations and the possible impact of birds. (Bas Tolsma)*

Bottom: *Rear view of a 747-400. Note the APU (auxiliary power unit) exhaust at the tail end. An APU is a device that provides energy for functions other than propulsion, including the electrical systems of the aircraft. (Bas Tolsma)*

A freshly maintained and cleaned 747-400 gleams in the sun. The cockpit with the hump behind it is a popular photo motif for many Jumbo enthusiasts. (Bas Tolsma)

the lighting provided. A wide-angle 10mm lens proved a must-have, inside the aircraft but also outside. Closeup shots from the outside are wonderful but the surroundings of the aircraft make for a powerful photo. One example is the aircraft sitting on jacks. To photograph a floating landing gear is one thing; to see that the entire aircraft behind it is suspended is a great catch.

"Hangar lighting posed a challenge. The reflections on the skin can be a true hassle when trying to get that one perfect picture. I would often have to move around to make sure that the reflections from the ceiling lights would not cover any logo or eye-catching detail. In contrast is photography under the wings and fuselage while in the hangar, which felt more like nighttime photography, playing with flash and shutter speeds. For every great picture I would also end up with about 20 unusable ones.

"The 747 was my introduction to photography and it sure taught me how to use both ends of the shutter speed and aperture ranges. The camera gear used was mid-range, affordable, and great for using in a hostile maintenance environment. It did what it had to do, documenting for classroom use, but it did so amidst grease, fuel, and dust. One thing I always made sure of was

situational awareness; it's easy to forget about your surroundings while looking through the viewfinder. Safety first.

"When it became more of an art, I ran into some limitations of the camera, mainly lighting issues. The photos would need some basic editing afterwards, mainly contrast and brightness corrections but I would always stay close to the original image.

"Flight deck photos can become a challenge due to the many shadows, backlighting and, if installed, the older CRT [cathode-ray tubes] screen refresh rates.

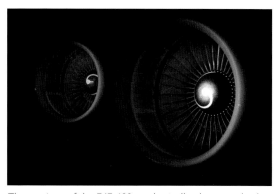

The engines of the 747-400 aesthetically photographed. The contrast between the dark background and the metal surface emphasises the engine blades. (Bas Tolsma)

A Jumbo lands at sunrise. The sun draws the contours of the distinctive 747 hump. (Bas Tolsma)

On one occasion, I tried to document some engine and system parameters during a high-power engine test run while sitting in the jump seat. The photos were to be used in class in order to show temperatures, valve positions, and pressures of the environmental control system. I took some test photos before the engine start, made some adjustments on the camera and was satisfied with the result. My experience with engine test runs was limited to lower thrust settings, not knowing what to expect at takeoff power settings. After engine start and runup, the throttle lever was advanced to the takeoff detent. I never expected that much shaking and bouncing in our seats; it made taking decent photos nearly impossible. I quickly resorted to faster shutters speeds, resulting in darker pictures due to less light. The major problem, however, was that I captured a crisp, unshaken picture, but the parameters on the displays weren't completely showing in my photos due to the refresh rate of the screens. It looked like the flickering you sometimes see while filming a display. I ended up stitching multiple photos together in order to get a usable picture for my students. I think I can now imagine what it would be like to read instruments during heavy turbulence."

Special Flights

Operation *Babylift* (1975)

With the central Vietnamese city of Da Nang having fallen in March 1975, and with Saigon under attack by North Vietnamese troops, the defeat of South Vietnam and the end of the war was just a question of time. On April 3, U.S. President Gerald R. Ford, petitioned by various aid agencies, announced Operation *Babylift*, a mass evacuation of children (most of them orphans) from South Vietnam to the United States and other countries (including Australia, West Germany, France, and Canada) on a series of flights aboard Lockheed C-5A Galaxy and Lockheed C-141 Starlifter cargo aircraft operated by the U.S. Air Force.

When American businessman Robert Macauley learned that it would take longer than planned to evacuate the children due to the lack of military transport planes, in particular after the first flight of a Lockheed C-5A Galaxy had crashed with the loss of 138 lives, he decided to charter a Pan Am Boeing

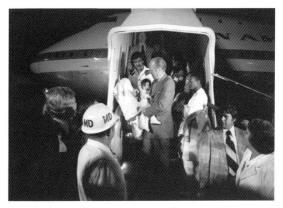

U.S. President Gerald R. Ford greets the children, nurses and crew members arriving on the Pan Am Jumbo in San Francisco on April 5, 1975. (U.S. National Archives)

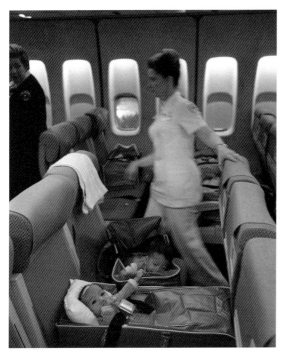

Nurses and Vietnamese refugee children on an Operation Babylift flight, probably the Pan Am 747, upon its arrival at San Francisco International Airport. (U.S. National Archives)

747 and arranged for 300 orphaned children to leave the country in early April, paying for the flight by mortgaging his own house. The orphans were gathered in Saigon, flown across the Pacific Ocean to Los Angeles and then Long Beach, California.

Lana Noone, co-author of *Children of the April Rain*, the first ever play about Operation *Babylift*, had adopted one of the Vietnamese orphans to be evacuated and longed for her safe arrival in the United States: "When Operation *Babylift* commenced, my husband Byron and I were awaiting the arrival of our daughter Heather Constance Noone from Vietnam. We were overjoyed to hear that President Ford had signed an executive order allowing the orphans to enter the United States without waiting for individual visas. Then, when the Lockheed C-5 Galaxy that evacuated orphans crashed this tragedy led us to believe our daughter had perished. That night President Ford appeared on TV saying that Operation *Babylift* would continue and

he would welcome the next plane. This was a Boeing 747, and he and Mrs Ford did meet it in San Francisco. I believe our daughter Heather was on that plane as we know she left Vietnam on the same day the 747 was used. However, due to her critical medical condition, she was taken off the plane at Clark Air Force Base in the Philippines and then went on to be hospitalised at Long Beach Naval Hospital, California, so we don't know if she continued on a 747 all the way to San Francisco. I am deeply grateful to the entire crew of the 747. These children were in harm's way and all those who sacrificed so much to bring them to their forever homes have my tremendous gratitude and appreciation."

The U.S. Air Force flights continued until artillery attacks by North Vietnamese Army and Viet Cong military units on Tan Son Nhut Airport (Saigon) rendered aircraft operations impossible. By the final American flight on April 26, over 3,300 infants and children had been evacuated, although the actual number has been variously reported. The Jumbo has contributed to this achievement. Along with Operation *New Life*, more than 110,000 refugees were evacuated from South Vietnam at the end of the Vietnam War.

Operation *Solomon* (1991)

During May 24-25, 1991, more than 14,300 Ethiopian Jews were flown from Addis Ababa to Israel in just 36 hours. This Israeli operation was called Operation *Solomon* (*Mivtza Shlomo* in Hebrew). Among the aircraft involved was a Boeing 747 from the Israeli airline El Al, which broke the world record for the most passengers on an aircraft: at least 1,078 people (possibly more) were on board.

Ethiopia had been embroiled in a civil war, with civilians living in extreme danger and hunger, and hundreds of thousands had fled to neighbouring Sudan. For some time Ethiopian Jews had sought to escape to Israel. However, Ethiopia's president, Mengistu Haile Mariam, would allow emigration only in exchange for Israeli weapons and American aid.

Meanwhile, Israeli, and American Jewish agencies in Ethiopia agreed that the advance of rebel forces toward Addis Ababa posed grave danger to the city's residents, and that as soon as Mengistu changed his mind, the Jews of Ethiopia should be quickly removed from the country. Covert plans were initiated to evacuate them at a moment's notice.

On May 21, President Mengistu fled into exile. Two days later, U.S. President George H. W. Bush sent a letter to the new president, Tesfaye Gebre Kidan, encouraging him to allow the Jews to leave Ethiopia all at once. He agreed, and by the next day Operation *Solomon* commenced. Addis Ababa fell to the rebels just a few days later, confirming that the speed of the operation indeed saved lives. Hundreds of people were involved in planning and executing Operation *Solomon*, including officials of Israel's Ministry for Foreign Affairs, The Jewish Agency for Israel, Mossad, the Israel Defense Forces (IDF),

the American Joint Distribution Committee (JDC), the United Jewish Appeal (now part of Jewish Federations of North America), the American Association for Ethiopian Jews, Keren Hayesod, and many more.

In the weeks leading up to Operation *Solomon*, The Jewish Agency oversaw the identification of those Ethiopians who were eligible to 'make *Aliyah*' (immigrate to Israel as new citizens) and arranged transfers, under security, to the Israeli embassy. Hundreds of buses were used to transfer immigrants to the airport. The use of El Al aircraft and the buses was made possible in part due to the fact that May 25, 1991 was a Saturday, the Jewish Sabbath, when travelling is prohibited by Jewish law and public vehicles generally lie idle; however, Jewish law encourages travelling on the Sabbath when it is for the purpose of saving lives.

In Addis Ababa, a *New York Times* reporter, who would join one of the night flights, noted that just off the runway, hundreds of

Left: *El Al's Boeing 747 (registered as 4X-AXF), which was used for Operation Solomon, among many other aircraft. (Hajime Suzuki)*

Right: *Ethiopian Jews on board one of the many planes on the flight to Israel. (Government Press Office of Israel / Alpert Nathan)*

passengers were sitting in small groups, separated by glow-in-the-dark ropes, each wearing a numbered sticker so as to keep track of each passenger. El Al airliners, with their Stars of David painted over, were lined up waiting to take on passengers. Before taking off, each pilot waited until another plane had returned from Israel to start his own flight. When signalled, the passengers boarded their respective planes, carrying only their children or small bags. At one point, 28 aircraft were in flight simultaneously.

Among the 35 planes used were Israeli Air Force C-130 Hercules military transports, El Al Boeing 747s, El Al Boeing 707s, and one Ethiopian airliner. On those flights whose seats had not been stripped, the passengers were packed two or three to a seat. Each flight carried immigrants, crew members, doctors or paramedics, and IDF soldiers.

The record-setting aircraft was an El Al 747-258C, registered as 4X-AXF. The maximum capacity for this craft is normally 480 people. It was possible to cram in at least 1,078 people thanks to several factors: the removal of seats, the passengers carrying no luggage, their numbers consisting of many children and babies, and the unfortunate fact that many passengers were malnourished and had low body weights and dimensions.

The New York Times reporter wrote: "At the airport this morning, it was difficult to tell who was more joyful – the ... Ethiopians who cheered, ululated and bent down to kiss the tarmac as they stepped off the planes, or the Israelis who watched them aglow, marveling at this powerful image."

Several babies were born during the flights, including two on the record-breaking Boeing 747. Nurses waited on the tarmac in Israel to put the babies into incubators and sick passengers into waiting ambulances. In total, around 140 people were whisked to hospitals. The rest of the more than 14,300 passengers were taken to their transitional housing. The Jewish Agency for Israel is responsible for promoting and facilitating *Aliyah* (immigration to Israel) and providing resettlement and acculturation services to new immigrants.

The lifestyle that the Ethiopian Jews had left behind in Gondar and Addis Ababa was very different from the modern, industrial lifestyle of Israel in the early 1990s, and their culture shock was total. Many had never used a gas stove or a light switch before, and most had survived as subsistence farmers, and had no marketable skills to bring into Israel's labour force. Despite the support of organisations and individuals, their adjustment to their new lives was extremely difficult.

Aliyah from Ethiopia continues today, and around 150,000 Ethiopian immigrants now live in Israel. As a cultural subgroup, the Ethiopian-Israeli community has made great strides.

Successive generations have become more prosperous and today there are Ethiopian-Israeli politicians, diplomats, military officers, entertainers, writers, visual artists, reporters, lawyers, teachers, social workers, translators, and more. Some of those who came on Operation *Solomon* now work full time at the Jewish Agency, offering support to today's new immigrants. The aircraft and crews of El Al, among them several 747s, helped make this possible.

Incidents and Accidents

Since its introduction in 1970, the Jumbo has been involved in some 160 aviation accidents and incidents, leading to 63 hull losses and causing more than 3,700 fatalities. Half of these hull losses resulted in no loss of life. A hull loss means that the aircraft has either been destroyed or has been damaged beyond economical repair. Some of the ones declared damaged beyond economical repair were older jets that had sustained relatively minor damage. Had these aircraft been newer, it might have been economically viable to repair and return them to service. There have also been several hijackings of Boeing 747s, such as Pan Am Flight 73 in 1986, hijacked by four terrorists, causing 51 deaths.

Tenerife Disaster (1977)

This tragedy occurred on March 27, 1977, and remains the deadliest accident in aviation history. 583 people died when a KLM Boeing

747-200 attempted to take off without clearance, and collided with a taxiing Pan Am Boeing 747-100 at Los Rodeos Airport on the Canary Island of Tenerife, Spain. The KLM jet sped down the runway unaware that the Pan Am 747 was still there. When the KLM captain saw the other aircraft, he tried to leapfrog the takeoff, almost made it, but chopped off the other jet's entire upper deck section and parts of the lower deck. The KLM jet skidded to the end of the runway and burned in a fiery blaze, killing all 248 people on board, while 61 of the 396 people on the Pan Am aircraft survived.

Pilot error from the KLM aircraft was the primary cause. Owing to a communication misunderstanding, the KLM captain thought he had clearance for takeoff. Another cause was dense fog, meaning the KLM flight crew was unable to see the Pan Am aircraft on the runway until immediately prior to the collision. The accident had a lasting influence on civil aviation. An increased emphasis was placed on using standardised phraseology in ATC communication by both controllers and pilots alike, thereby reducing the risk of misunderstandings. The Pan Am jet involved in this tragedy was *Clipper Victor*, which was the first 747 to fly commercially. In its first year of service, it also became the first 747 to be hijacked in 1970.

Wreckage of the KLM Jumbo De Rijn on the runway after the Tenerife airport disaster of March 27, 1977. (Nationaal Archief: Collection Anefo/929-1005)

The KLM Boeing 747-206B De Rijn destroyed in the collision. (GMP)

Korean Air Lines Flight 007 (1983)

On September 1, 1983, a Korean Air Lines Boeing 747-200 was en route from Anchorage, Alaska, to Seoul, South Korea. Due to a navigational mistake made by the flight crew, the airliner deviated from its

The Sukhoi Su-15 was a Soviet-made twin-engine interceptor. One such aircraft shot down the Korean Air Lines 747. (U.S. Air Force)

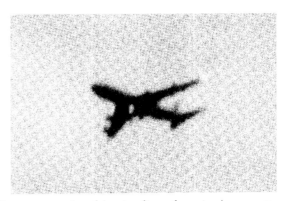

Left: *After the recovery of the wreckage of Air India Flight 182, a reconstruction of the aircraft on a frame in a hangar was carried out to determine the cause of the accident. (U.S. Federal Aviation Administration)*

Right: *This last known photo taken from the ground of Japan Airlines Flight 123 clearly shows the absence of the vertical stabiliser. (Japan Transport Safety Board/CC BY 4.0)*

original planned route and flew through prohibited Soviet airspace. The Soviet Air Force considered the unidentified jet to be a U.S. spy plane, so a Sukhoi Su-15 interceptor shot down the 747 with air-to-air missiles. Depending on the source, the Su-15 pilot had fired warning shots beforehand, but the 747 crew probably had not noticed them. The Korean airliner eventually crashed in the sea near Moneron Island in the Sea of Japan. All 269 people aboard were killed. The Soviets located the wreckage on the seafloor on September 15, and eventually found the flight recorders in October, but this information was kept secret until 1993.

The Soviet Union initially denied knowledge of the incident, but later admitted shooting down the aircraft, claiming that it was on a spy mission. The U.S. government accused the Soviet Union of obstructing search and rescue operations and the subsequent investigation. The flight recorders were released ten years later, after the dissolution of the Soviet Union. As a result of the incident, the United States altered tracking procedures for aircraft departing from Alaska. In addition, it prompted the Reagan administration to allow worldwide access to the United States global positioning system (GPS).

Air India Flight 182 (1985)

On June 23, 1985, a bomb exploded on an Air India 747-200 operating on the Montreal–London–Delhi route. The aircraft crashed off the southwest coast of Ireland, killing all 329 people on board, including 268 Canadian, 27 British, and 24 Indian citizens. The bombing of this flight is the largest mass killing in Canadian history, the deadliest aviation incident in the history of Air India, and the deadliest act of aviation terrorism until 9/11. The Babbar Khalsa terror group was implicated in the bombings.

Japan Airlines Flight 123 (1985)

On August 12, 1985, a Japan Airlines Boeing 747SR en route from Tokyo to Osaka suffered a sudden decompression and crashed near Mount Osutaka, 62 miles (100 kilometres) from Tokyo. The subsequent investigation concluded that the rapid decompression was caused by a faulty repair after a tail-strike incident during a landing at Osaka Airport in 1978. The 747's rear bulkhead had been repaired with an improperly installed doubler plate, compromising the jet's airworthiness. Cabin pressurisation continued to expand and contract the improperly repaired bulkhead until the day of the crash, when the faulty repair failed, causing a rapid decompression that ripped off a large section of the vertical stabilizer and caused the loss of hydraulic controls to the entire jet. With 520 of the 524 people on board killed (some died of their injuries hours later waiting for help), it is the deadliest single-aircraft accident in aviation history.

Left: *A Pan Am Jumbo similar to the jet hijacked by the Abu Nidal organisation. (U.S. National Archives)*
Right: *The demolished cockpit of Pan Am's* Clipper Maid of the Seas, *which crashed over Lockerbie, Scotland, after a bomb on board exploded. (Air Accident Investigation Branch/National Archives UK/OGL V2.0)*

Pan Am Flight 73 (1986)

On September 5, 1986, a Pan Am 747-100 was en route from Bombay, India, to New York with scheduled stops in Karachi, Pakistan and Frankfurt, West Germany. After arriving from Bombay with 388 people on board, the jet was hijacked while on the ground at Karachi by four armed Palestinians of the Abu Nidal Organisation. A grand jury later concluded that the hijackers were planning to use the jet to pick up Palestinian prisoners in Cyprus and Israel. The 17-hour-long hijacking came to an end when the hijackers opened fire on the passengers at 9.30 p.m. local time, but soon ran out of ammunition, resulting in some passengers fleeing the jet through the emergency exits. Special forces of the Pakistan military responded by storming the jet and seizing the hijackers. Depending on the source, 51 passengers were killed during the incident, including nationals from India, the United States, Pakistan, and Mexico. All the hijackers were arrested and sentenced to death in Pakistan. However, the sentences were later commuted to life in prison.

South African Airways Flight 295 (1987)

On November 28, 1987, a South African Airways Boeing 747 Combi en route from Taipei, Taiwan to Johannesburg, South Africa, with a stopover in Mauritius, experienced a catastrophic in-flight fire in the cargo area, broke up in midair, and crashed into the Indian Ocean east of Mauritius, killing all 159 people on board. During an extensive salvage

operation one of the black box recorders was recovered from a depth of 16,100 feet (4,900 metres). Although a cargo of fireworks was blamed, the official investigation was unable to determine the cause of the fire, thus leading to conspiracy theories.

Pan Am Flight 103 (1988)

On December 21, 1988, a Pan Am Boeing 747-100, the *Clipper Maid of the Seas*, was en route from Frankfurt to Detroit via London and New York City, when it was blown up by a bomb over Lockerbie, Scotland. The explosion went off under the letter 'P' in the black Pan Am logo. This severed the front of the jet from the rest of the fuselage. The 747 smashed into Lockerbie, killing 11 people on the ground and all 259 people on board. It is the deadliest terrorist attack in the history of the United Kingdom. Following a three-year investigation, arrest warrants were issued for two Libyan nationals in November 1991. In 1999, Libyan leader Muammar Gaddafi handed over the two men for trial at Camp Zeist, Netherlands, after protracted negotiations and UN sanctions. One was jailed for life but released in 2009 by the Scottish government after being diagnosed with prostate cancer. He died in May 2012 as the only person to be convicted for the attack.

United Airlines Flight 811 (1989)

On February 24, 1989, a United Airlines Boeing 747-100 en route from Los Angeles to Sydney, with stopovers in Honolulu and Auckland, experienced the failure of the front cargo door in flight shortly after leaving Honolulu. The resulting explosive decompression blew out several rows of seats, resulting in the deaths of nine passengers. The jet returned to Honolulu, where it landed without further loss of life. The U.S. National Transportation Safety Board (NTSB) determined in 1992 that the probable cause of the accident was the sudden opening of the cargo door, which was attributed to improper wiring and deficiencies in the door's design.

El Al Flight 1862 (1992)

On October 4, 1992, an El Al 747-200F cargo aircraft departed New York for a flight to Tel Aviv, Israel via Amsterdam in the Netherlands. At 2.40 p.m. local time, it made a stopover landing at Amsterdam-Schiphol Airport. The aircraft took off again at 6.28 p.m., and as it was climbing, engine No. 3 and its pylon separated from the wing and collided with engine No. 4, causing this engine and pylon to separate as well. An emergency was declared and the crew acknowledged their intention to return to Schiphol. While reducing speed in preparation for the final approach, control was lost and the aircraft crashed into an 11-floor apartment building in the Bijlmermeer suburb of Amsterdam.

A total of at least 43 people were killed, including the jet's three crew members, a passenger in a jump seat, and at least 39 people on the ground. The subsequent investigation concluded that the cause of the separation of engine No. 3 was the failure of one of its fuse pins. This was proven by the examination of the torn-off engines later found in the Gooimeer (Gooi Lake). In this case, there was a material defect or a fatigue fracture, which should have been detected during routine inspections, but was not. Serious damage was also caused to the right wing's leading edge. The loss of hydraulic power and damage to the wing prevented the flaps from functioning properly, so this, combined with the loss of two engines, caused the aircraft to a stall and crash. This accident is the deadliest aviation disaster to occur in the Netherlands.

Trans World Airlines Flight 800 (1996)

On July 17, 1996, a TWA Boeing 747-100 en route from New York to Rome via Paris exploded and crashed into the Atlantic Ocean near East Moriches, New York. All 230 people on board died in the crash. The four-year NTSB investigation concluded that the probable cause of the accident was the explosion of flammable fuel vapours in the centre fuel tank. Problems with the aircraft's wiring were found, including evidence that the fuel quantity indication system (FQIS) was malfunctioning. As a result of the investigation, new requirements were developed to prevent future fuel tank explosions. For almost 25 years, the wreckage of Flight 800 was kept by the NTSB and used as an accident investigation teaching aid.

Recovery of wreckage from the TWA-800 flight from the seabed. (U.S. Dept. of Defense)

Charkhi Dadri Mid-Air Collision (1996)

On November 12, 1996, a Saudi Arabia Airlines Boeing 747-100 en route from Delhi, India to Dhahran, Saudi Arabia collided with a Kazakhstan Airlines Ilyushin Il-76 en route from Chimkent, Kazakhstan to Delhi, over the village of Charkhi Dadri, around 62 miles (100 kilometres) west of Delhi. The crash killed all 349 people on board both planes, making it the deadliest midair collision in aviation history and the deadliest aviation accident in India. The subsequent investigation could not determine the exact cause of the collision, but found evidence of various factors that contributed to it, one being (depending on the source) the lack of collision avoidance equipment on board the Ilyushin Il-76. The Directorate General of Civil Aviation subsequently made it mandatory for all aircraft flying in and out of India to be equipped with an airborne collision avoidance system. This accident set a worldwide precedent for mandatory use of the traffic collision avoidance system.

China Airlines Flight 611 (2002)

On May 25, 2002, a China Airlines Boeing 747-200 en route from Taiwan to Hong Kong disintegrated in midair and crashed into the Taiwan Strait, 23 nautical miles (43 kilometres) northeast of the Penghu Islands, killing all 225 people on board. The final investigation report found that the accident was the result of fatigue cracking caused by improper repairs to the aircraft after a tail-strike incident 22 years earlier. The accident is the deadliest in Taiwanese aviation history.

British Airways Flight 149

A Boeing 747 (G-AWND), known as British Airways Flight 149, made headlines on its way from London-Heathrow to Sultan Abdul Aziz Shah Airport in Kuala Lumpur, Malaysia, when it made its fateful stopover in Kuwait on August 2, 1990.

After the aircraft arrived at Kuwait International Airport, outside Kuwait City, the flight never resumed due to ongoing events on the ground. Prior to the 747's arrival, the neighbouring state of Iraq had launched a full-scale invasion of Kuwait in the early morning. Within hours, Iraqi army units had reached Kuwait City and taken control of the airport. As a consequence, the 747, its passengers and crew were captured by Iraqi troops, with most of them initially held in several nearby hotels with other foreigners under armed guard. The British Airways jet was later destroyed on the ground under unclear circumstances.

Helen Peters, one of the flight attendants on BA Flight 149, recalls the tumultuous and traumatic experience: "Thursday, August 2, 1990 – this date will forever be etched in my memory as one that changed my life forever. I was preparing for my evening trip

Helen Curtin as a British Airways flight attendant. (Helen Peters)

on BA Flight 149 to Kuwait, when I heard a reporter on the news state that 100,000 Iraqi troops were massing on the border of Iraq and Kuwait. After checking in for the flight, the question was asked to the CSD [Cabin Service Director]: will we still fly to Kuwait? The crew were assured that we would be monitored via satellite and if there were any changes on the border the flight would divert immediately. Feeling reassured, we boarded the flight ready to prepare the plane for the passengers when we were informed there was a problem with the APU system which then caused a two-hour delay. We eventually departed and the flight went smoothly with no reports of troops crossing the Iraq-Kuwait border. Flight 149 arrived in Kuwait at approximately 4:15 a.m.; passengers disembarked and we were on our way to the hotel, ready for a well-deserved sleep. It was a few hours later when I was

woken by our CSD who explained that Iraq had invaded Kuwait and the runway had been bombed – we wouldn't be flying out anytime soon. Looking out of the window, I could see soldiers surrounding the hotel and the sound of gunfire could be heard close by. Soldiers had taken over the fifth floor and rooftop of the hotel, the Kuwait Regency Palace.

"The next day the crew managed to telephone home before the lines were cut – this was the last time we could communicate with our friends and families. Some of the passengers of Flight 149 had to sleep in the corridors and on sofas as there weren't enough beds in the airport hotel. The crew were taking turns to feed and look after all the passengers, who were becoming a bit anxious, adding to the fact that no one had any change of clothes or toiletries. Eventually some of the crew were allowed to board the plane to retrieve cabin bags; the smell was unbearable and the bars and duty free had been ransacked. Later in the day, some passengers and crew from the airport were transported to our hotel, where we met them in our uniforms, cheering and clapping as they entered the foyer – relief showed all over their faces.

"Many incidents happened over the 18 days whilst being held hostage in the Kuwait Regency Palace Hotel. For me, a few encounters will always stay in my memory, one being the feeling of sheer terror when all hostages in the hotel were locked in the dining room and surrounded by armed guards. Terrified that we would all be shot, my hands started to shake and tears welled up. The soldiers were searching every room, looking for any Kuwaiti resistance.

"Twelve days later would be my next daunting experience. We were called to our captain's room for an emergency meeting and told that the troops were starting to move and hostages would be split up and used as human shields. We would try to escape and hide in a 'safe house', which had been arranged through

Top: *Newspaper clipping about the hostage taking. Helen is second from right.* (Evening Standard)

Bottom: *The destroyed British Airways Jumbo lies strewn on its apron at Kuwait International Airport.* (U.S. National Archives)

Helen Curtin's (Helen Peters') personal record of her experiences during her time as a hostage. (Helen Peters)

a friend of the captain's. We were to meet up at 2 p.m. in the lobby. Soldiers were starting to come into the hotel – it seemed movement was happening a lot quicker. Another stewardess and I managed to grab a bag from our room and headed to an underground ballroom where we wait until 2 p.m. We stayed in the dark, hiding under a stack of tables and chairs. Suddenly we heard someone come in. I could feel my heart thumping in my chest. We were terrified of being discovered by a soldier. After a few hours we left and went looking for the captain – only to find out he and five others had escaped with only the clothes they were standing in.

"The next day we were separated into groups, our passports taken from us and then we were put onto a number of buses. That would be the last time I saw some of the crew until our freedom flight home, and this would be the first time in 18 days that we travelled outside of the hotel. There was so

much devastation around, buildings turned to rubble and cars blackened by fire – so sad to see Kuwait, now a broken city. Our next stop was a university campus, which was being used as a military HQ. Hundreds of Iraq soldiers were dotted around the grounds. We were told to sit inside a lecture hall and waited for hours until an army captain came in and proceeded to ask us to split up into four groups of twelve. My group was herded onto a military bus where boxes of ammunition lay at our feet; sparks could be seen coming from the engine, which made us all feel very concerned. Our final destination was only a few miles from the hotel – the Salmiah Palace, which was located across from a beach, obviously one of the strategic points.

"When we drove up to the palace, I noticed that it was surrounded by a large number of troops camping outside. Once inside we met up with British and American people who had been working in Kuwait but had been rounded up and held hostage. We were fed and managed to find some clothes to change into. Later the captain in charge wanted to have photos taken of himself with his captives. He sat on a sofa in between another stewardess and I; a soldier took our photo and then the captain wanted a group shot as well. Our time there was very short, as in less than 24 hours we would be on the move again.

"The journey, although hot and stuffy, lasted only 30 minutes. We arrived at the Palace of Salem Alsabah, where we met up with another group of crew and passengers. We were now 44 in total – two of them were children. It was quite surreal being held captive in a luxury palace which had been trashed by the soldiers. Drawers lay smashed and empty on the floor, broken glass was everywhere, the whole building turned upside down. By the end of the day the mess was somewhat cleared up, but we faced another dilemma we had no water. We were now 19 days being held captive and had no means of knowing what was really happening in the outside world.

We settled into the palace, finding rooms to sleep in, either a bed, a sofa or the floor. We found out that some of the hostages had skills we might be able to use – electronics, computers, cooking. I was delegated the residential hairdresser, setting up a salon in one of the bathrooms. Food was rationed and mainly consisted of rice with gravy, consumed on gilt-edged chinaware with gold-plated cutlery. Spending time outside was limited; occasionally we would be allowed out for 30 minutes. One day I noticed a tank with its gun barrel pointing out to sea, and on top sat a red and white beach umbrella – quite a bizarre sight. Temperatures outside were exceptionally high as it was now peak summer, reaching over 100°F, around 40°C Then the air

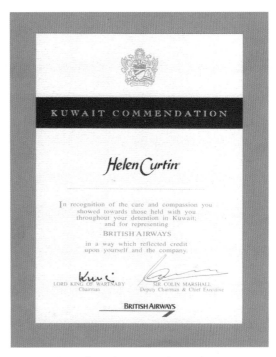

Commendation for Helen Peters (then Helen Curtin) from British Airways for her commendable conduct during her time as a hostage. (Helen Peters)

conditioner broke down, leaving us living in extreme heat day and night.

"We had now stayed in the palace for 11 days – today would be a significant day. We were called to a meeting with an Iraqi captain, who explained to us that all women and children were to be released. He was holding our passports and a list of names, which he called out. We were told that we had 15 minutes to get our belongings together. One of the children, a young boy, was crying and shouting at the soldiers, 'Let my daddy go with us,' he sobbed.

"Saying goodbye to the men was very emotional; telephone numbers and quickly scrawled messages were passed to the women. We were counted up and in turn given our passports, then boarded a waiting bus. We waved goodbye to the men not knowing when or if we would see them again. The bus left at about 1:30 p.m. and proceeded to pick up more women

Newspaper headline about the release of the hostages. (Evening Standard)

and children. Our first stop was at a white house where we met up with a group who had been with us at the university. We waited inside as it was so much cooler as there was no air conditioning on the bus. I asked one of the soldiers for some food as I hadn't eaten since the day before. We were given some dry biscuits, chocolate, and water to share around. We left the white house for another pickup but this time we had to stay on the bus, which by now was sweltering. At the next, and final, stop I recognised some of the male crew members from Flight 149. Then, at 4 p.m. our journey started on the long, dusty road to Baghdad.

"We drove through the devastated city, buildings turned into rubble, cars and buses blackened by fire, and tanks scattered all around, their burned-out shells all that remained. It was so surreal. We arrived at the Iraqi border where we stayed for a while. We were told we had a choice of either going to Basrah or straight to Baghdad. We chose to drive through the night to Baghdad as it would be a lot cooler. It was a long and dusty drive with many stops along the way. During one of the stops the driver bought a melon from a vendor, and stood outside the bus eating it. We were all so hungry and thirsty but none was passed to us.

"It was beginning to get light as we approached the city of Baghdad; soldiers were patrolling the streets, tanks poised with their gun barrels pointing to the sky. It was early morning when we arrived at the Al-Mansour Melia Hotel – it had taken 16 hours' travelling by bus. We were told that we would be leaving the next day on Iraq Airlines. In the meantime, we were given food and a room to sleep in. Soldiers were positioned outside in the corridors. Most of the female crew members and passengers of Flight 149 had also joined us at the hotel, so we swapped stories

about the many different places we had been held as 'human shields'.

The next day we left the hotel and arrived 20 minutes later at Baghdad Airport where hordes of camera crews from around the world swamped with questions about our captivity in Kuwait. I gave an interview to CNN, which was broadcast around the world – little did I know my family would see me on TV for the first time in a month. After going through passport control, another stewardess and I asked if we could look around the Iraq Airlines 747 that would be flying us home; we spoke to the crew and asked if we could arrange for all the British Airways crew to sit together, preferably at the front of the aircraft. They made this possible, which was such a nice gesture. We would have to wait a bit longer before the doors closed as we were waiting on Jesse Jackson, the American civil rights activist who had negotiated the release of the women and children hostages. When he arrived, he gave us a wave, to which we all responded with a cheer. The doors were closed and we were on our way to Paris and then to the United Kingdom. Tears welled up as we hurtled down the runway. I couldn't believe we were leaving after 31 days of captivity and we would finally soon be back home."

Helen Peters had joined Britannia Airways in 1982 as a cabin crew member working on the Boeing 737 for a year, after which she flew for British Caledonian Charter on the DC-10. She then applied to British Airways and was finally accepted on November 11, 1984, working on the 747. After her traumatic experience in the First Gulf War of 1991, she transferred to short haul which entailed flying on the 737, the 757, and the Airbus A320. During Helen's time on short haul, she decided to work part-time flying three days a week, as support crew. Eventually, when she was pregnant with her third child, she felt it was her time to hang up her wings, and left British Airways on March 31, 1998.

THE JUMBO
IN MUSEUMS

A Boeing 747 as a large exhibit in a museum or as a public attraction is always a centre of attention. Now that this proud and majestic aircraft will be seen less and less often in the skies, the preserved Jumbos in museums will help ensure that its history will remain alive for many years to come.

(Corendon Hotels & Resorts)

CHAPTER 6

Long Live the Queen

By Ted Huetter
(The Museum of Flight, Seattle)

At the opening ceremony of The Museum of Flight's Great Gallery in 1987, then-Vice-President George H. W. Bush said, "one can imagine ... someday a 747 displayed at this museum." Two years later, Boeing offered the museum the first Jumbo ever built, RA001, named *City of Everett*. And on March 28, 1990 the 21-year-old workhorse was officially accessioned into the museum's collection. The 'Queen of the Skies' was a major coup for the growing museum at Boeing Field. This historic plane brought status, which in turn helped lure other aviation and space treasures. But there was no gallery for it, great or otherwise: RA001 was a hangar queen without a hangar.

During that time, the museum was restoring its aircraft in a rented facility at Paine Field in Everett, Washington (RA001's hometown). The museum's leadership saw that owning the place could enhance tourism and provide better use of the facility. But money was tight. Then Boeing calls – the company wants to put RA001 back into service as a testbed for the never-flown engines on the new 777 in development. A lease-back arrangement is signed, and the Queen comes out of retirement.

The deal proved fortuitous for the aerospace giant when the test engine caught fire on its first 747 flight, giving ample time for engineers to work out the kinks before the Triple Seven's maiden flight in 1994. Meanwhile, the lease-back fees allowed the museum to take ownership of the restoration grounds in Everett.

RA001's lease to Boeing expired in 1995. But there still wasn't room on the museum campus, so the plane domiciled at the airport about a mile north of there, becoming more of a landmark for passing motorists than for museum visitors. Finally, in 2002, the museum opened an expansive, asphalt-paved airpark across the street from its galleries. RA001 had a home, joined by a British Airways Concorde, the first *Air Force One* jet, the Boeing 737 prototype, and other large planes

The newly restored City of Everett *in its original 1969/70 appearance in the late afternoon sun. (Ted Huetter)*

Top Left : *The restored interior of the upper deck in the hump, in the typical look of the late 1960s. (Ted Huetter)*

Middle Left : *View of the cockpit where test pilots Jack Waddell and Brien Wygle and flight engineer Jess Wallick once sat down to write aviation history with this prototype. (Ted Huetter)*

Then in 2012, *Seattle Times* writer Ron Judd published a Sunday feature story describing RA001's sad condition in lurid but loving detail: "The World's No. 1 Jumbo Jet Languishes, Looking for a Savior." The article became a call to action. Aviation technicians offered to volunteer their time and experience to help restore the ageing artifact, while others pledged funding. The museum devised a plan. Two years later the plane was almost like new.

"As far as I know," said then-Museum of Flight Curator Dan Hagedorn, "this is the largest aircraft that has ever been restored inside and out where she sits." The objective was not to merely bring the aircraft back to the end of its service life in 1990, but to its beginning. "We really want to retain the 1969/70 character of the aircraft." Missing and damaged equipment

For comparison: the distinctive nose section (above) before restoration and after (below). The restorers even affectionately repainted the logos of the 26 airlines that had pre-ordered the 747 in the 1960s. (Ted Huetter)

in the collection. The Queen assumed a commanding presence and was a major draw for tourists and aviation enthusiasts.

Despite regular, valiant efforts to preserve RA001, they were no match for Seattle's infamous climate. With each year the Queen looked wearier, tarnished, faded, and even mossy. After decades of being a standout, she was now blending in with the dark, slippery environment. It was on the brink. Restoration of the plane would take millions of dollars and several years. Adoring fans were plentiful, monied patrons were few.

Following its extensive restoration, the jet once again appears in its former glory – just as it did on the day of its rollout in 1968. Today, the famous aircraft has a weather-protected and covered stand. (Ted Huetter)

Ted Huetter is an aerospace writer and photographer. He is an avid pilot, and since 2008, he has been the Senior Public Relations and Communications Manager at The Museum of Flight in Seattle. (tedhuetter.com)

was replaced from an eclectic variety of sources spanning the globe. Some 15,000 sheets of sandpaper were used to prepare the exterior for repainting – complete with the airline logos that adorned the nose on its maiden flight. Thousands of parts were cleaned, polished, repaired, and painted. Even unused vintage airline upholstery was found to replace the threadbare fabric on the upper-deck lounge furniture.

The restoration of RA001 also helped secure funding for an enormous new pavilion that would replace the airpark and protect all of the museum's large aircraft from Seattle's liquid sunshine. The Aviation Pavilion opened in 2015. And the dazzling Queen, surrounded by her ancestral family, contemporaries, and even today's 787 Dreamliner, reigns supreme.

Yankee Mike's Journey to a New Home

Hermann Layher (President of the Sinsheim and Speyer Technik Museums)

The Boeing 747 set up in lofty heights is one of the main attractions of the Technik Museum Speyer. From the Jumbo, which is placed on a 20-metre-high stand, visitors get a good view of the museum grounds and the neighbouring city of Speyer. The left wing can be walked on. (Technik Museum Speyer)

Watch Video:
747 Museum

"Today it is enthroned 20 metres [66 feet] above the ground in the Technik Museum Speyer – our Boeing 747-200. But the way it was brought to us was certainly not easy as the Jumbo was to present many challenges. But I can reveal one thing in advance – the effort and expense that this aircraft cost us was worth it.

"But let's start from the beginning: 'our' Boeing 747-200 (serial number 21588; registration D-ABYM) was delivered to Lufthansa from Boeing's Everett plant on October 20, 1978 for a purchase price of 125 million marks. Just a few days later, on November 1, the first regular passenger flight was made from Frankfurt to Boston and Philadelphia. Later, Margot Stoltenberg, widow of former Prime Minister Gerhard Stoltenberg, christened the Jumbo the *Schleswig-Holstein*.

"In the course of her career, *Yankee Mike* completed a total of approximately 96,000 operating hours with 16,373 takeoffs and landings.

"But how did she actually become 'our' Jumbo? The Technik Museum Sinsheim Speyer consists of two privately run museums (Sinsheim and Speyer, both located in southwest Germany), which pay all their own operating costs and are supported by the Förderverein (Friends' Association) Auto-Technik-Museum e.V., which has some 3,500 members worldwide. It is only thanks to this large network and the participation of our members that we have been able to obtain this super bird. Our supporters and fans contribute numerous ideas and put a wide variety of museum activities into practice. One of our association members worked at Lufthansa Technik at that time and informed us early and before it was publicly announced that a Jumbo was about to be retired and (like many other 747-200s) was also to be scrapped. After contacting the airline, we managed to acquire it for the symbolic price of one euro.

"Now we were faced with the almost insoluble task of how to transport *Yankee Mike* to our museum in Speyer. With a length of 70.5 metres [231 feet], a wingspan of 59.6 metres [196 feet], and a height of 19.3 metres [63 feet], as well as an empty weight of about 172 tonnes, the only conceivable way was actually by air. However, the runway directly next to our museum at Speyer was too short. The solution to the transport problem thus represented the greatest challenge for us up to that point, but at the same time it was to become our museum's greatest masterstroke.

"Together with our workshop team, our friends, and partners from the Scholpp company and the forwarding agency Kübler, we worked out a transport plan. On January 28, 2002, the big day arrived: grey, low-hanging clouds lay over the Karlsruhe/Baden-Baden Airport, which was the closest Jumbo-suitable airport for *Yankee Mike*'s final landing and was about 90 kilometres [56 miles] away from the museum.

"About 40 minutes after takeoff from Frankfurt Airport, two landing lights flashed through the grey clouds. The aircraft flew in almost silently. To give it a fitting farewell, *Yankee Mike*'s crew did not go directly into the landing approach, but flew over the field at a low altitude, pulled up steeply, banked and landed after this lap of honour. This final touchdown not only marked the end of the career of this Boeing 747-200; its captain and co-pilot also retired after this ferry flight.

"After landing, Lufthansa technicians removed more than 1,000 components from the aircraft to return them to the airline's

For the complicated transport of the Boeing 747-200 to the museum, the wings, the horizontal stabilisers and rudder had to be dismantled. (Technik Museum Speyer)

Close-up of the moment when one of the two wings is detached from the aircraft fuselage. (Technik Museum Speyer)

Transport of the Jumbo on the Rhine. Many people lined the banks to watch. (Technik Museum Speyer)

material cycle. These included the four powerful General Electric engines and various smaller components.

"Since further transport had to be partly by road and water, we decided to disassemble *Yankee Mike* into several parts and then reassemble it at Speyer. She was thus to be the first large aircraft that would be completed again after disassembly and displayed in a museum. During this phase, we received wonderful support from Lufthansa.

"The next step was to load the approximately 70-metre-long (231 feet) fuselage and the other parts onto low loaders. For the subsequent drive to the NATO ramp on the banks of the Rhine near Söllingen, the local authorities had to remove several traffic signs, unhook power lines and remove street lamps. Once we arrived at the

Rhine, the next challenge awaited us. Days of heavy rainfall had led to high water. *Yankee Mike* was therefore unable to drive onto the pontoon on her low loader as planned, but had to be lowered completely onto the pontoon surface. This was an exciting and time-consuming procedure.

"Early on Sunday morning, March 24, our Jumbo finally travelled on the Rhine. In order to pass the lock at Iffezheim, the pontoon had to take on an additional several hundred tonnes of water for a greater draught. Until reaching the bridge at Germersheim, water had to be continuously pumped out of the ballast tanks so that the pontoon was not too deep in the water, while at the same time the fuselage could still fit under the bridge. The transport on the Rhine became a task of 'millimetre precision' that took a whole day.

Thanks to the experienced transporters, the huge aircraft fuselage also took tight turns without suffering or causing damage. (Technik Museum Speyer)

After removing all the control surfaces, the aircraft looked like a giant tube. (Technik Museum Speyer)

"In the natural harbour near Speyer, at a tributary of the Rhine, conditions were cramped. This required the felling of trees and the creation of aisles and a temporary road for the low loaders and aircraft parts. The following day, thousands of spectators lined the roads (that were closed to traffic) in Speyer during the exciting final transport section as no one wanted to miss the spectacle. It took our team a whole day to cover the distance from the banks of the Rhine to Speyer, as challenges also awaited us in the city area.

"At the Speyer fire station, the curves were so tight that we initially feared we would have to hoist the fuselage over the fire station using giant cranes. Finally, however, we managed to manoeuvre it around the obstacles. At our museum we had already demolished a building as a precaution because of the Jumbo's size.

"After arriving safely, Easter 2002 marked the beginning of *Yankee Mike*'s eight-week reassembly. We wanted to set up our new 172-tonne super bird with its landing gear extended at a height of 20 metres [66 feet], so that it would be clearly visible from a distance. In addition, it was to be made accessible to our museum visitors. Therefore, we first had to have foundations made for the girder structure and supports. As an engineer and technology enthusiast, I did not miss the opportunity to make my contribution to this and therefore took over the construction.

"We made the interior of the Jumbo more interesting by partially dismantling the cover panels, thus providing a good impression of the complex interior of such a widebodied aircraft and its enormous dimensions. Another feature that is unique worldwide is that we made the cargo hold and the left wing accessible. I had the idea for the latter during a flight to the U.S., when I was sitting a bit cramped in my seat and, looking at the large wings, thought, 'Gee, there's so much space out there, it's too bad you can't use that area.'

"Just over a year after the Jumbo's arrival at Speyer, the time had come: on a bright and warm morning, three huge cranes lifted our freshly cleaned *Yankee Mike* onto her stand. On April 18, 2003, we finally opened her to visitors. Since then, the aircraft has proved a unique experience for people from far and wide, and we are very proud of it.

The reassembled Jumbo is hoisted onto its stand with the help of cranes. (Technik Museum Speyer)

Dipl. Ing. Hermann Layher is the president of the Technik Museums Sinsheim and Speyer and a long-time classic car enthusiast. (Arturo Rivas/© Motor Klassik)

The last 'takeoff' of the proud Jumbo. (Technik Museum Speyer)

'Touchdown' on the frame: the Jumbo has reached its final stationary position. (Technik Museum Speyer)

"Even today, I take my hat off to my workshop people as they took apart a very complex aircraft to an extent that no one had ever done before – not even the manufacturer Boeing itself. Years later, the company approached us about a project, to draw on our experience in aircraft disassembly.

"Although we did not have to meet all the requirements for reassembly that are necessary for flight operations, it was nevertheless a demanding task to restore the Jumbo to such an extent that it would be able to withstand the dynamic demands placed on it as an outdoor exhibit in the long term: after all, the forces of strong gusts of wind acting on the huge vertical stabiliser and the approximately 600-square-metre (6,500-square-feet) wings that cause these components to bend, should not damage *Yankee Mike*.

"Without the support of the many helpers and authorities (as well as a certain willingness to take risks on the part of the companies involved), this complex transport operation would not have been possible as originally planned. It could only be mastered because we pulled together. This included our association members, since the museum is their hobby and contributing their personal strengths is a matter of honour. Because there is a world beyond money that is characterised by reliability, camaraderie, and solidarity and therefore makes such projects possible. This is what the museum means to me, and this is what drives me and my work. While our member Heinz Rössler of Kübler

Spedition (transport) donated the services of his company, other members financed the work of the structural engineers as well as the use of the crane. The Rhine transport operation involved a return cargo load, so we only had to pay for the fuel. Since we, as a privately run, non-profit museum, received the Jumbo for the symbolic price of one euro, we were able to keep the total acquisition costs within reasonable limits. My thanks therefore also go to Lufthansa, which became an honorary member of our museum after this project. Their trust in us was so great that they left their *Yankee Mike* to us and allowed us to disassemble her for transport. This appreciation has to be valued even more as no one had ever done this before us.

The extravagantly illuminated 747-200 (D-ABYM) at night. The jet is visible over several kilometres by day and night. (Mark Broekhans)

"Our Jumbo at Speyer is particularly important to me. Our responsible handling of this sensitive, large-scale exhibit also made it possible to obtain the very precious Concorde from Air France, which is now enthroned at Sinsheim, thus proving once again that we are capable of carrying out such large-scale projects. We are very proud of this achievement."

Visiting the Jumbo

By Jean-François Louis (Association des Amis du Musée de l'Air, Le Bourget, France)

"The Boeing 747 (ex-Air France F-BPVJ) on display at the Musée de l'Air et de l'Espace at Le Bourget near Paris was the first aircraft through which I guided visitors as a volunteer docent. Usually, the guided tour starts in front of the airliner. Here I always ask the visitors about their first impression when looking at the massive aircraft. The answers vary depending on whether or not my guests are used to air travel, and especially whether they have had the opportunity to fly on an Airbus A380.

"For those who are not so familiar with widebody jets, the Jumbo's imposing size is the first matter of surprise. For those for whom the A380 is the visual reference, size is not an issue. Regardless of the dimensions, it is above all the conspicuous hump behind the cockpit that makes the aircraft recognisable as a Jumbo jet to almost all visitors. This feature gives it a unique profile, which sometimes causes children to compare its appearance to a bat. A funny idea. "After boarding the aircraft, we enter the First Class, which is partially deprived of its seats. Here, everyone becomes aware of the imposing size of the Jumbo, the first aircraft with two aisles, capable of carrying some 400 passengers – a quantum leap forward compared to its 180-seat predecessor, the Boeing 707. And everyone is surprised to learn that the manufacturer Boeing considered the Jumbo only as an interim solution until the introduction of the supersonic Boeing 2707, whose development, however, was cancelled in 1971. With more than 1,500 aircraft built since 1970, the Jumbo has in fact revolutionised long-haul air transport and democratised this mode of travel that was previously only reserved for the privileged

An Air France 747-100 very similar to the one preserved at the Musée de l'Air et de l'Espace (National Air and Space Museum) at Le Bourget. (Air France Museum)

The Jumbo F-BPVJ on display at the Musée de l'Air et de l'Espace is a Boeing 747-100 that was delivered to Air France in 1973 and retired in 2000. Three years later, it became one of the museum's largest artefacts. The museum is one of the world's finest aviation museums, both for the wealth of its collections and long history. It features an incredible collection of more than 400 aircraft, 150 of which are on display, including planes from early pioneers, both world wars, experimental jets, one Boeing 747 and two supersonic Concordes. (Musée de l'Air et de l'Espace/Frédéric Cabeza)

Interior of the 747-100. Visitors can explore the cabin during the guided tour or on on their own. (Musée de l'Air et de l'Espace/Alexandre Fernandes)

Museum and Association des Amis du Musée de l'Air (AAMA) volunteer and aviation enthusiast JeanFrançois Louis. (Jean-François Louis)

rich. Many are also surprised to learn that this machine was designed back in the mid-1960s.

"The 'wow effects' for visitors are in fact multiple as few are aware that the Jumbo introduced various innovations including the luggage and cargo loading system by container. Its enormous dimensions

Some of the ceiling and wall cover panels as well as some sections of the floor have been removed to provide a unique view of the complex interior of a Jumbo and its enormous dimensions. (Musée de l'Air et de l'Espace/Alexandre Fernandes)

The Boeing 747-400, former KLM aircraft, City of Bangkok, made her first commercial flight in June 1989. After 30 years of service it found a new final destination: the backyard of the garden of Corendon Village Hotel, Amsterdam. (Corendon Hotels & Resorts)

Turning a Jumbo into a waterpark may be one of the most spectacular methods of preserving an aircraft. This 747-100 flew until 2010, when it was retired. It was then craned to the top of the Wings and Waves indoor water park building at the Evergreen Aviation Museum in McMinnville, Oregon, and turned into a waterslide. Over the years, many Jumbos have become exhibits in museums or attractions around the world. More will be added in the future. (Carol M. Highsmith Archive/U.S. Library of Congress Collection)

forced airports to completely rethink their organisation to accommodate aircraft with a wingspan of 60 metres [197 feet], which is 15 metres [50 feet] more than that of the Boeing 707, thus requiring enlarged and redesigned parking spaces, modified check-in points and boarding areas for more than 400 passengers. This meant that existing airport structures that had been built since 1958 (when the Boeing 707 entered service) now had to be adapted to handle more than twice the passenger volume, not to mention the number of airport employees which also had to double. Moreover, the giant new aircraft required costly investments in equipment such as higher gangways, more powerful tractors, taller firefighting trucks, and increased fuel stock capacity.

"I then lead the group into the centre section of the cabin, where many covers and panels have been removed to show visitors the aircraft's design structure, with the wire control cables for the elevators and rudder visible under the cabin ceiling causing particular astonishment. How can it be that in a 'modern' aircraft these controls are not electric? A child once said to me, 'Well, these wire cables look like the brakes on my bicycle!'

"When our tour ends in front of the imposing landing gear after exiting the jet, everyone goes home convinced that the Boeing 747, the first giant in the sky, is indeed the aircraft that has made international air travel affordable to virtually everyone."

The Jumbo Becomes Architecture: The 747 Wing House

If houses could fly, the Wing House in Malibu, California would undoubtedly be the Jumbo among them. Built by architect David Hertz and his Studio of Environmental Architecture for a private client, the residence has a unique design and offers an idyllic panoramic view of the Pacific Ocean and the Santa Monica Mountains.

Most striking is the roof structure of the two-part home, completed in 2011, which is made of real wings from a decommissioned Boeing 747-200. This jet was in service for TAP Air Portugal,

The main house comprises two separate buildings linked together and uses two wings and two horizontal stabilisers from a Boeing 747-100. The 747 Wing House is an unconventional building in the Santa Monica Mountains. (David Hertz Architects)

Close-up of the wingtip with the former radio antenna. (David Hertz Architects)

TWA, and Tower Air between 1972 and 1993. With dimensions of about 125 feet × 46 feet (38 × 14 metres) each, they allow for a large-scale, self-supporting structure. Approximately $30,000 was the cost of the entire jet, which was waiting to be scrapped in the desert. The parts were delivered by helicopter.

The result is a one-of-a-kind residence that was even registered with the aviation authorities to prevent confusion with a crashed aircraft. In addition to its special design, the house also boasts a high sustainability value, since in addition to the wings, many parts of the fuselage, tail unit, and engine nacelles were also used in the construction. As a successful example of recycling materials, the Wing House has won the California Council's Residential Design Award, among others.

THE END
OF AN ERA

For millions of people, the Jumbo has always been a special means of transport. Former test pilot Brien Wygle sums it up: "The 747 was always in a class by itself, it was a great triumph, and we have every right to be proud of it."

(Andrey Babin)

CHAPTER 7

During the development of the Jumbo in the 1960s, only four-engined propeller-driven aircraft such as the then still-active Douglas DC-4 or Lockheed L-1049 Super Constellation, as well as the modern four-engined jets of the Boeing 707, Douglas DC-8, de Havilland DH. 106 Comet, and Vickers VC10 types, could fly medium- and long-haul routes.

At that time, the thrust of four engines was needed to sufficiently power heavy aircraft for long-haul flights. They were also a safety factor to keep the aircraft in the air in case of failure of one or two engines. Aircraft with two engines, such as the Boeing 737, the Douglas DC-9, the BAC 1-11, and the Sud Aviation SE 210 Caravelle, operated primarily on short- or medium-haul routes at the time. Although they could fly over the Mediterranean, for example, they could not fly long distances over the Atlantic or the Pacific.

Most of the major American and international passenger airlines have been using a 'hub-and-spoke' system to route their aircraft traffic. A hub is a large central airport that flights are routed through, and spokes are the routes that aircraft take out of the hub. The spokes are the destinations that aircraft fly to from the hub airport. The hub-and-spoke system became the norm for most major airlines in the late 1970s. The previously used point-to-point system required airlines to fly directly between two small markets. This resulted in many flights that were very often half empty, causing airlines to lose money. Today, most airlines have at least one hub, a central airport, that their flights have to go through. From that hub, the spoke flights take passengers to select destinations. A good example of a hub-and-spoke system is that of the American carrier Delta Airlines, located at Hartsfield-Jackson Atlanta International Airport, Georgia. With about 1,000 flights a day to 225 domestic and international destinations, it is the world's largest airline hub. For example, if a passenger wants to travel from Charleston, South Carolina to Memphis, Tennessee, he would face the problem that there is not a lot of demand for a direct Charleston–Memphis flight. As a result, the airline first flies the passenger from Charleston to Atlanta, and then from Atlanta to Memphis via a connecting flight.

Unique, distinctive and iconic: the silhouette of the 747 bathed in the golden light of a sunset. (Furkan Borakazi)

Several airlines use Florida's Orlando International Airport as a hub. For many years, the 747 transported large numbers of passengers from one hub to another. From there, travellers boarded smaller aircraft to reach their final destination. Today, smaller but more economic twin- and three-engined jets enable passengers to fly directly from point to point, thus making a stopover at a 747 hub unnecessary. (Paul Aranha)

The hub-and-spoke system was created to save airlines money and give passengers better routes to their destinations. The operation of a fleet of aircraft is expensive, and every flight has certain set costs. Each seat on the plane represents a portion of the total flight cost. For each seat that is filled by a paying passenger, an airline lowers its break-even price, which is the seat price at which an airline stops losing money and begins to generate a profit on the flight. The 747 with its large number of more than 350 seats was able to reduce the price for each seat compared to previous four-engined jets such as the 707 carrying just half the number of passengers. For many years, the 747 made it possible to transport large numbers of passengers from one hub to another. From there, travellers had to switch to a smaller aircraft to reach their final destination.

With the introduction of smaller but more economic twin- and three-engined jets, it became possible to fly passengers directly from point to point, thus making a stopover at a hub (using a 747) unnecessary. International flights bypassing traditional hub airports and landing at smaller cities became more common in the late 1980s and early 1990s, thus slowly but gradually eroding the 747's original market. However, many international airlines continued to use the Jumbo on transpacific long-haul routes.

For many years, the Jumbos of international passenger airlines met at the world's major airports. This era is now gradually coming to an end. (Swissair/ETH-Bibliothek Zürich/LBS_SR04-012114/CC BY-SA 4.0)

In recent years, however, things have continued to change to the disadvantage of the 747 and the '3 Mots' such as the Lockheed L-1011 TriStar and McDonnell Douglas's DC-10 and MD-11. In the meantime, even smaller 'twins' of the types Boeing 777 and 787 or Airbus A350 have the range of a Jumbo. Even the normal cruising speed, which has always been above average for the 747, can now be flown by these modern aircraft. These higher speeds are an important factor on extreme long-haul routes, since a crew's maximum flight duty time is of course also limited. They are also now allowed to operate up to five hours from the nearest airport. This means they can cross vast oceans like the Atlantic and even the Pacific on great circle routes. At the time, this direct routing was still a 'privilege' of the '4 Mots'. Today, '2 Mots' are only capable of such long flights because of the development of modern and particularly safe engine technologies.

The low fuel consumption of '2 Mots' and the resulting lower maintenance requirements have reduced operating costs for the airlines enormously. Thus, nonstop long-haul flights from Amsterdam to Buenos Aires or from Singapore to London with twin-engined aircraft are the 'new normal'.

Top Left: *The German Condor was the world's first leisure airline to use the Jumbo, starting in 1971. It not only flew to the Far East but also to Mallorca, Malaga or Las Palmas during summer. With room for almost 500 seats, this lowered ticket prices and thus helped make vacation trips to sunny destinations affordable for the masses. (Condor)*

Top Right: *A few years ago, some All Nippon Airways (ANA) aircraft, such as this 747-400, were painted on the outside with characters and motifs from the very popular Pokémon video games and decorated on the inside with various Pokémon themes for promotional purposes. (Yoshiharu Mohri)*

Bottom Left: *The 747's service ceiling is 45,100 feet (13,746 metres). Although this is not enough to reach the moon, the 747 can fly slightly higher than the Airbus A380, which makes it to about 43,000 feet (13,100 metres). (Andrzej Kostrzewa)*

Bottom Right: *A 747 with the moon in the background. The former US airline Pan Am advertised in the 1980s with the slogan 'First in space'. Although the company alluded to space travel, it wanted to draw attention to the enormous legroom on board their grey planes. (Ron Stella)*

Top: *Besides its service as a passenger jet, airlines from various countries utilise their Jumbos as flying symbols of national pride. These memorable flights take place with the country's aerobatic display. Here, the Red Arrows, pride of the British Royal Air Force, are flying in formation with a British Airways 747, which is painted in the 1970s retro look of BOAC, the predecessor of British Airways. (Manuel Acosta Zapata).*

Bottom: *Alpha Jets of the Patrouille de France, the French Air Force's aerobatic squadron, in formation flight with an Air France 747. In 2020, this airline also decided to bring forward the retirement of its costly jumbo fleet due to the Coronavirus crisis. (Armée de l'Air et de l'Espace/M. Jouary)*

In the coming years, smaller jets such as the recently developed Boeing 737 MAX or the new Airbus A321XLR will also increasingly enrich international and transoceanic air transport. They can very efficiently fly long-haul routes with low passenger demand. While the demand for the Jumbo is falling, the availability and capability of medium-sized, and now smaller, twin engined airplanes, have completely changed long-haul aviation.

By 2005, the Jumbo was no longer in a class of its own: Boeing's European rival Airbus had built its own oversized airliner, the A380. Designed as a double-decker, it can carry up to 853 passengers. As with the 747 before it, airports had to adapt to its enormous size. As early as the mid-1990s, Boeing was considering various further developments of the 747-400 to counter potential competition from the A380, which was then under development. However, after no customers were found for these new variants of the Jumbo, Boeing ended its 747X or 747X stretch plans and presented the Sonic Cruiser instead. This was a concept of a jet

Top Left: *The Spirit of Australia (747-400) from Qantas. The longest nonstop flight by a 747 lasted 20 hours, 9 minutes and 5 seconds. This occurred in 1989 on the 18,001-kilometre (9,720-nautical-mile) route between London and Sydney. The aircraft was Qantas' City of Canberra (a 747-400 with registration VH-OJA), which is now on display at the Historical Aircraft Restoration Society in New South Wales. For five decades, the Jumbo enabled the Australian airline to connect Down Under with the rest of the world. During the Coronavirus crisis, the airline retired its 747 fleet. (Akira Uekawa)*
Top Right: *A United Airlines 747 taking off over a populated area. In 2018, United became the last major American airline to retire its passenger Jumbos. Delta Airlines had already decommissioned its jets the previous year. American Airlines has not even owned a 747 since the 1990s. (Gabor Hajdufi)*

Bottom Left: *British Airways was one of the largest operators of the Jumbo. The 747-400 flew, for example, the prestigious route from London to New York, or to Johannesburg, South Africa. At times, the airline had more than 30 Jumbos in its fleet. During the Coronavirus crisis, the airline decided to take them all out of service. (John Powell)*

Bottom Right: *In 2018, Lufthansa chose its visually stunning 747-8 to present the airline's redesigned livery to more than 3,000 guests. (Lufthansa)*

KLM Royal Dutch Airlines (Koninklijke Luchtvaart Maatschappij) operated about ten Jumbos until the start of the Coronavirus pandemic, but all of these were taken out of service during the crisis. (Gabor Hajdufi)

Left: The 747 is capable of transporting its cargo to virtually anywhere in the world within 24 hours. Without efficient cargo aviation, modern world trade would be less efficient, as transoceanic transport is far more time-consuming. (Jerry Pang)

Right: Due to the Coronavirus crisis and the resulting decline in international air traffic, many airlines have mothballed or completely retired their expensive Jumbos (and other aircraft types). (Gabor Hajdufi)

airliner distinguishing itself from conventional airliners by its delta wing and high-subsonic cruising speed of up to Mach 0.98. As airlines generally preferred lower operating costs over higher speed, Boeing ended the Sonic Cruiser project in 2002 and shifted to the slower but more fuel-efficient 7E7 (later named 787 Dreamliner) airliner.

The terrorist attacks of September 11, 2001, led to a crisis in commercial aviation as people temporarily lost confidence in the security of international air travel. After the business had recovered in 2004 and new, more fuel-efficient engines were under development, Boeing presented a plan for a more economical and quieter Boeing 747 variant under the name Boeing 747 Advanced. This was to be the answer to the Airbus A380 in order to maintain Boeing's position as the leading manufacturer of widebody aircraft against its European rival. Since demand for a passenger variant had declined noticeably in the meantime, Joe Sutter's assumption that the aircraft would one day be needed as a freighter has come true, since there was still a need for high-performance freighter aircraft. Boeing therefore offered the new jet as a freighter from the outset. Officially designated 747-8, this variant was unveiled on November 15, 2005. While the 747-8F freighter version sold immediately, Boeing received an order from Lufthansa for more than 20 units of the 747-8 Intercontinental passenger variant (including options) but only when a further fuselage extension with the associated capacity increase had been done at the end of 2006.

In the meantime, the market for the 747 has shrunk significantly. Boeing has recorded around 150 orders for the current 747-8/-8F version since 2005 (as of the end of January 2021). Airlines also took more 747s out of service than they placed new orders for. By 2013, the global 747 fleet had shrunk to about 685 aircraft. Some 15 years earlier, the airlines were still flying more than 1,000 Jumbos.

After the events of 9/11 plunged international air travel into a crisis due to fears of further hijackings, the 2020/1 Coronavirus pandemic caused a longer-term crisis with deeper implications for air travel, airlines, and the aircraft manufacturing industry. With ticket bookings plummeting, many passenger aircraft were grounded, while numerous jets took off only partially full, generating no profit, only losses. This crisis particularly affected large four-engine jets, such as the 747 and the Airbus A380 and A340, which are expensive to operate and maintain,

Although several airlines had been gradually phasing out their Jumbos for years (the older 747-100/200/300 variants first) and replacing them with modern twin-engined jets such as the Boeing 777 and 787 and the Airbus A350, the Coronavirus pandemic hit the Queen of the Skies (as well as the A380 and A340) with undisguised force, so that many 747 operators such as Air France, KLM, Virgin Atlantic, Qantas, and British Airways (the largest 747 operator at the time) took it out of service completely within weeks or months, and either sold or scrapped the jets. The gradual and graceful retirement of the grand old lady had now given way to an abrupt end of service. Just a few airlines, including Lufthansa, Air China, and Korean Airlines, decided to retain the 747-8 and some of the older 747-400 variants in their fleets. With a total combined fleet of some 50 Jumbos (primarily freighters), Atlas Air is the world's largest operator of this fleet type. One 747-400 passenger variant is used for VIP service (N263SG).

After a success story of more than 50 years, with over 1,500 aircraft delivered, the last 747 will leave the Everett plant in the foreseeable future. Due to a lack of orders, Boeing recently announced the end of production. The Queen of the Skies broke records and established standards that we take for granted today, but which were still considered unattainable in the 1960s. Over the years, it has cemented its place in the world as a cultural and revolutionary icon that the Airbus A380 will never match. While the A380 has taken its place in the world as a superlative aircraft that boasts numerous innovations, it has not truly revolutionised aviation the way the Boeing 747 did.

Legacy of the Jumbo

By Michael Lombardi (Boeing Senior Corporate Historian)

Every day millions of people fly – it is an accepted way of life – but that has not always been the case. From the early days of commercial aviation, flying was limited to business travellers and those with the means to purchase the very expensive tickets. Destinations were also limited, requiring a number of connections to fly between major cities.

In 1969, that all changed as the Boeing 747, called the 'Super Jet', and dubbed the 'Jumbo Jet' by the press, took to the skies for

Michael Lombardi started at Boeing in 1979 and has been the senior corporate historian since 1994. He has a BA in history from City University and has presented lectures on aerospace history to the American Institute of Astronautics and Aeronautics, the Royal Aeronautical Society, and several air museums. As the author of a book about the history of strategic airpower and a Boeing spokesperson, Mr Lombardi has appeared in numerous documentaries. He also serves as the guest curator for The Museum of Flight, Seattle, and is a fellow of the Royal Aeronautical Society. (Bob Ferguson)

the first time. To those who have loved the plane through the years she is the 'Queen of the Skies'.

The 747 was created by the men and women of Boeing, from brilliant engineers to highly skilled machinists using imagination, courage, hard work, dedication, and, above all, passion. They were called 'The Incredibles' and their pioneering spirit and amazing accomplishment still inspires the latest generation of Boeing employees.

The 747 introduced a number of technological and aviation firsts, the greatest being the invention of the twin-aisle, widebody design; it also marked the first commercial use of the high-bypass turbofan engine. Beyond size, comfort, and efficiency what is most important to the flying public today is safety. Under the command of chief designer Joe Sutter, the 747's design was based on safety. Boeing introduced quadruple hydraulic systems, redundant structures and four main landing gears (the plane is able to operate on

two). Boeing also reinvented pilot training, moving away from strictly procedural training to behavioural training.

It did not take long for the 747 to make a giant impact on air travel. It was the must-have flagship for the world's airlines and attracted passengers with its luxury and passenger appeal. But it was the Super Jet's size, world-spanning range, capacity, and economy that had the greatest impact, making it possible for all of humanity to fly, and with that the 747 will forever mark the point in history when any person on planet earth could fly anywhere on the globe. By July 1970, one million passengers had flown on the 747 - the Super Jet was shrinking the world.

The 747's size and its distinctive hump make the plane readily recognisable. That distinctive shape is a result of the art that is inherent in great engineering; its design is often recognised as an outstanding work of architecture. The jet has also become a part of popular culture starring in numerous movies, TV shows, and in the lyrics of songs.

Over the many decades since the 747 was born, jet engine technology has advanced considerably. The original JT9D engines that powered the first 747s produced 43,000 lb of thrust each and to make a giant plane that could span the globe required four engines. Today the GE9X engines that power the new 777X family produce 134,300 lb of thrust each and with much less fuel burn. The simple fact is that the efficiency of the twin-engined 777 has eclipsed the four-engined passenger aeroplane. The feature that will be difficult to replace is the unique First Class and Business Class experience especially in the upper deck – this feature and the mystique of the Queen of the Skies continue to make it the first choice as an airline flagship.

The 747 will continue to provide a service that the original designers foresaw, optimizing the design to perform as a freighter. That foresight to reinforce the flight deck, optimise the interior for cargo, and to place the flight deck above the main deck to allow efficient loading through the nose of the plane ensured that the Queen will be

After its unique career in the history of aviation, with more than 1,500 built, the Jumbo is now entering its twilight years. (John Powell)

with us for decades to come as arguably the world's finest freighter – a testament to an aeroplane that was built to last.

Over the last five decades, the 747 has become legendary. Today it is a bridge to a romantic era of flight, an era that we should continue to aspire to resurrect. But more than that, the 747 is a reminder of the power of the human spirit and what we can accomplish with our hearts, minds, and hard work; it reminds us that even though we may lose

hope in a world that seems filled with strife, we can turn our eyes to the skies and see those great contrails of the Queen of the Skies crossing the heavens and know that we can still overcome great adversity and accomplish incredible things.

"The 747 was always in a class by itself, it was a great triumph, and we have every right to be proud of it."

Brien Wygle

APPENDICES

Appendix A

Boeing 747 Orders and Deliveries by Year
(Source: The Boeing Company)

Year	Total	2021	2020	2019	2018	2017	2016	2015	2014	2013	2012	2011	2010	2009	2008	2007	2006
Orders	1,573	2	- 1	-	18	6	18	6	2	13	7	3	1	5	2	16	53
Deliveries	1,561	1	5	7	6	14	9	18	19	24	31	9	-	8	14	16	14

Year	2005	2004	2003	2002	2001	2000	1999	1998	1997	1996	1995	1994	1993	1992	1991	1990	1989	1988	1987	1986
Orders	46	10	4	17	16	26	35	15	36	56	32	16	2	23	31	122	56	49	66	84
Deliveries	13	15	19	27	31	25	47	53	39	26	25	40	56	61	64	70	45	24	23	35

Year	1985	1984	1983	1982	1981	1980	1979	1978	1977	1976	1975	1974	1973	1972	1971	1970	1969	1968	1967	1966
Orders	42	23	24	14	23	49	72	76	42	14	20	29	29	18	7	20	30	22	43	83
Deliveries	24	16	22	26	53	73	67	32	20	27	21	22	30	30	69	92	4	-	-	-

Appendix B

Boeing 747 Orders and Deliveries to End April 2021
(Source: The Boeing Company)

Model Series	ICAO code	Orders	Deliveries		Unfilled orders
747-100	B741 / BSCA[1]	167	167	205	-
747-100B		9	9		-
747-100SR	B74R	29	29		-
747-200B	B742[2]	225	225	393	-
747-200C		13	13		-
747-200F		73	73		-
747-200M		78	78		-
747 E-4		4	4		-
747-300	B743	56	56	81	-
747-300M		21	21		-
747-300SR		4	4		-
747-400	B744 / BLCF[3]	442	442	694	-
747-400ER		6	6		-
747-400ERF		40	40		-
747-400F		126	126		-
747-400M		61	61		-
747-400D	B74D	19	19		-
747-8I	B748	48	47	143	1
747-8F		107	96		11
747SP	B74S	45	45	45	-
747 Total		1,573	1,561		12

1) BSCA refers to SCA (Shuttle Carrier Aircraft), used by NASA.
2) B742 includes the VC-25A, two 747-200Bs modified for the U.S. Air Force.
3) BLCF refers to the 747-400LCF Dreamlifter, used to transport Boeing 787 Dreamliner components

Appendix C

1) Boeing 747 Specifications

(Source: The Boeing Company)

Model	747SP	747-100	747-200B	747-300	747-400	747-8
Cockpit crew	3				2	
Typical seats	276	366		400	416	467
Cargo	3,900 cu ft (110 m³)	6,190 cu ft (175 m³)			5,655 ft³ (160.1 m³)	6,345 cu ft (179.7 m³)
Length	184 ft 9 in (56.3 m)	231 ft 10 in (70.66 m)				250 ft 2 in (76.25 m)
Cabin width	239.5 in (6.08 m)					
Wingspan	195 ft 8 in (59.6 m)				211 ft 5 in (64.4 m)	224 ft 7 in (68.4 m)
Wing area	5,500 ft² (511 m²)				5,650 sq ft (525 m²)	5,960 sq ft (554 m²
Wing sweep	37.5°					
Tail height	65 ft 5 in (19.9 m)	63 ft 5 in (19.3 m)			63 ft 8 in (19.4 m)	63 ft 6 in (19.4 m)
MTOW (Maximum Takeoff Weight)	700,000 lb (317.5 t)	735,000 lb (333.4 t)	833,000 lb (377.8 t)		910,000 lb (412.8 t)	987,000 lb (447.7 t)
OEW (Empty Weight)	337,100 lb (152.9 t)	379,500 lb (172.1 t)	375,100 lb (170.1 t)	384,000 lb (174 t)	412,300 lb (187.0 t)	485,300 lb (220.1 t)
Fuel capacity	50,359 US gal 190,630 l	48,445 US gal 183,380 l	53,985 US gal 204,360 l		63,705 US gal 241,150 l	63,034 US gal 238,610 l
Turbofan ×4	Pratt & Whitney JT9D-7 or Rolls-Royce RB211-524 or GE CF6				PW4000 / CF6 / RB211	GEnx-2B67
Thrust ×4	46,300–56,900 lbf 206–253 kN	43,500–51,600 lbf 193–230 kN	46,300–54,750 lbf 206.0–243.5 kN	46,300–56,900 lbf 206–253 kN	62,100–63,300 lbf 276–282 kN	66,500 lbf 296 kN
MMo (Maximum Operating Mach number)	Mach 0.92					Mach 0.9
Cruising Speed		econ. 907 km/h (490 kt), max. 939 km/h (507 kt)			933 km/h (504 kt)	
Range	5,830 nmi 10,800 km[1]	4,620 nmi 8,560 km[2]	6,560 nmi 12,150 km[2]	6,330 nmi 11,720 km[3]	7,670 nmi 14,200 km[4]	7,730 nmi 14,320 km[5]
Takeoff	9,250 ft (2,820 m)	10,650 ft (3,250 m)	10,900 ft (3,300 m)	10,900 ft (3,300 m)	10,700 ft (3,260 m)	10,200 ft (3,100 m)

1) JT9D, 276 passengers
2) JT9D, 366 passengers and baggage
3) 400 passengers and baggage
4) PW4000, 416 passengers and baggage
5) 410 passengers and baggage

NOTES

[1] *Airways* magazine, 2013

[2] ibid.

[3] ibid.

[4] ibid.

[5] ibid.

[6] ibid.

[7] speakers' event, The Museum of Flight, 2014

[8] ibid.

[9] ibid.

[10] speakers' event, The Museum of Flight, 2014

[11] Boeing Radiation Health Protection Group, 1994 report

[12] speakers' event, The Museum of Flight, 2014.

[13] ibid.

[14] ibid.

[15] speakers' event, The Museum of Flight, 2014.

[16] *Honolulu Star-Bulletin,* January 22, 1970, p. D-16.

[17] Airways magazine, 2013

[18] ibid.

[19] ibid.

[20] 'Missile Defense Umbrella?' Center for Strategic and International Studies, January 11, 2011

A Jumbo takes off into the sunset, perhaps symbolic of the sunset of an illustrious and incomparable career of more than 50 years. (Gabor Hajduti)

SOURCES

Books

Bauernfeind, Ingo: *Concorde – Supersonic Icon*. Bauernfeind Press, Mülheim an der Ruhr, North Rhine-Westphalia, Germany (2019)

Jenkins, Dennis R.: *Boeing 747-100/200/300/SP – Airliner Tech Vol. 6*. Specialty Press, Forest Lake, Minnesota, United States (2000)

Sutter, Joe: *747: Creating the World's First Jumbo Jet and Other Adventures from a Life in Aviation*. HarperCollins, New York, New York, United States (2006)

Walsh, Kenneth T.: *Air Force One: A History of the Presidents and Their Planes*. Hyperion Books, New York, New York, United States (2003)

Presentations and Reports

Tillman, Mark W. (Colonel, U.S.A.F., ret.) about *Air Force One* on 9/11: *Wings & Things Guest Lecture Series* at the National Museum of the U.S. Air Force, Dayton Ohio, United States (February 2012)

Gallacher, Thomas D. about the use of depleted uranium in the construction of the 747: Report for the Oak Ridge National Laboratory: Boeing Radiation Health Protection Group (1994)

Sutter, Joe & Wygle, Brien, about building and flying the 747: Speakers' Event, The Museum of Flight, Seattle, Washington, United States (2014)

Telephone Interviews and Research by Author

Feuerstein, Mark (2020/1)

Hauke, Stefan (2020/1)

Huetter, Ted (2019/1)

Lombardi, Michael (2020/1)

Stockhoff, Sebastian (2020/1)

Wygle, Brien (July 2020)

Interviews

Sutter, Joe: Interview with *Airways* magazine (2013)

ACKNOWLEDGEMENTS

Joe Sutter, the father of the 747, once said, "I just had a great bunch of guys working with me." I can also say this with regard to the creation of this book because, as with the building of an aircraft, this could only happen with the cooperation and support of individuals, companies, and institutions. As a result, I am sincerely indebted to the dozens of Boeing 747 professionals and enthusiasts who consented to be interviewed and who submitted their personal experiences, recollections, and personal material.

I would like to express my special gratitude to Brien Wygle, Mark Feuerstein, Michael Lombardi, and Heather Anderson of the Boeing Company; Sebastian Stockhoff, Stefan Hauke, Birgit Horrion, Jan Netzeband, Maximilian Reuter, Dr. Patrizia Hey, Luisa Schürmann and Anja Stenger of Lufthansa; Patrouille de France; Armée de l'Air et de l'Espace and many more.

The following contributed vital information and material: Jean-François Louis, Alain Rolland, and Christophe Goutard of Musée de l'Air et de l'Espace, Le Bourget; Jean Signoret, Bernard Bazot, and Bernard Pourchet of the Air France Museum; Susanne Freitag/f2 KREATION from Air France; Ted Huetter from The Museum of Flight, Seattle; Hermann Layher, Rainer Schwald, and Simone Lingner from the Technik Museum Sinsheim/Speyer; Marcos Valdez, David Allen, Dan Reese, Francis Sheller, and John Winder from Global SuperTanker; Dr. Thomas Keilig of Deutsches SOFIA Institut (DSI); Doug Miller of the Pan Am Historical Foundation; Sarah Bronson from The Jewish Agency for Israel; El Al; Jim Davies of British Airways; Mark Bitterman of Stratolaunch; Johanna Tillmann of Condor; Dr. Christian Gelzer of NASA; Helen Peters; Paul Jeeves; John Powell; Bas Tolsma; Lana Noone; Jason Rabinowitz; Mary Kirby; *Airways* magazine; David Hertz Architects; U.S. Air Force/U.S. Air Force Museum; U.S. Department of Defense, and many more.

Special thanks and gratitude go to Dan Sharp and Steve O'Hara and and their colleagues at the Mortons Media Group for publishing the English version of this book as well to my family for supporting me in this and all my other creative endeavours.

Many thanks also to the following people: Chris Cocks for editing, Debashis Gupta for the layout and Dr. Andreas Hofmann, Steven Whitby, Marvin Goldman, Don Cooper, Dennis Smith, and my lifelong friend Lars Drachenberg, for general support. I also extend my appreciation to all the photographers who contributed to the visual content of this work. This book is for Tommy.

INDEX